RYA
Catamaran
Handbook

Written by Jeremy Evans

© RYA Catamaran Handbook
Copyright RYA 2007
First Published 2007

The Royal Yachting Association
RYA House, Ensign Way
Hamble, Southampton
Hampshire SO31 4YA

Tel: 0845 345 0400
Fax: 0845 345 0329
E-mail: publications@rya.org.uk
Web: www.rya.org.uk

ISBN 1905104405 RYA Order Code G46

All rights reserved. No part of this publication may
be stored in a retrieval system, or transmitted, in
any form or by any means, electronic, mechanical,
photocopying, recording or otherwise, without
prior permission in writing from the publishers.

C000088997

Acknowledgements

Jeremy Evans would like to thank Don Findlay from the International Formula 18 Class Association, Andy Webb of AW Sailboats, Neil 'Sanchez' Watts, Kristian Robertshaw and Steve Beard at the Hobie Cat Centre, the Nissan Hobie Team and Hobiecat Europe for their help with this book. Much appreciated!

Photo Credits

All photos by Jeremy Evans except: p1, p8/9, p80, p93, p104, p112/113, p128/129, p130/131 Nissan Hobie Team/Pierrick Contin; p18/19 Volvo Extreme 40 Oskar Kihlborg p21, p24/25, p62/63, p69 Hobiecat Europe/Pierrick Contin; p71 Ronde om Texel 2005/Van Kinderen & Kats Photography; p72, p90, p96/97 Nissan Hobie Team/Bernard Biancotto; p98 Ronde om Texel 2006/Pierrick Contin.

A CIP record of this book is available from the British Library.
Ring 0845 345 0400 for a free copy of our Publications Catalogue.

Totally Chlorine Free **Sustainable Forests** **EMAS** VERIFIED ENVIRONMENTAL MANAGEMENT

Published by **The Royal Yachting Association**
RYA House, Ensign Way, Hamble, Southampton SO31 4YA
Tel: 0845 345 0400
Fax: 0845 345 0329
Email: publications@rya.org.uk
Web: www.rya.org.uk

© 2007 Royal Yachting Association

All rights reserved.

Note: While all reasonable care has been taken in the preparation of this book, the publisher takes no responsibility for the use of the methods or products or contracts described in the book.

Cover design: Pete Galvin. Pictured are Richard Glover & Sam Rowles racing across Portland Bay, 2012 Olympic Sailing Venue
Typeset: Batt Creative
Proof-reading and indexing: Alan Thatcher
Printed by: Printed in China through World Print

Contents

Contents

Contents

Foreword

Welcome to the world of catamaran sailing, whether you are sailing for pleasure, leisure or racing at the highest level this sport has challenges for everyone. Catamaran sailing is both exhilarating and relaxing, with a constantly changing environment - no two races are ever the same. Despite winning 8 world championships I can still state I have not sailed the perfect race. The secret to my success is that sailing is still my sport, my passion and I love it.

Enjoy.

Darren Bundock
Tornado World Champion 1998, 2001, 2002, 2003.
Tornado European Champion 1999, 2002, 2003, 2004.
ISAF World Sailing Games Champ 2002, 2006.
Formula 18 World Champion 2004, 2005.

Website: www.darrenbundock.com

1 | Why sail a Catamaran?

A catamaran is a boat with two parallel hulls, unlike the more usual monohull, which has a single hull, or a trimaran, which has a single hull and two outer floats. The word 'catamaran' is derived from the early 17th-century Tamil kattumaram, which literally means 'tied wood'. It refers to the clever trick that native fishermen used to promote stability by attaching two canoes with wooden branches as an antidote to rolling around in a single canoe.

The first advantage of a catamaran is that by having two hulls held apart by beams, which are nowadays usually made from aluminium and carbon fibre, a catamaran is more stable than a monohull (single hull). The second advantage is that because the two hulls are spread apart, the boat will not be so ready to tip over when the sails are full of wind, and the crew have more leverage than on a single-hulled dinghy, allowing a catamaran to carry bigger and more powerful sails. The third advantage is that the slim hulls of a catamaran have far less wetted surface area (wetted surface area creates drag, which slows a boat down) than the much wider monohull of a dinghy, particularly when the windward hull (closest to the wind) is lifted clear as shown in the photo of Glenn Ashby and Darren Bundock (exchanging crew roles for a laugh) opposite. Compared to a keelboat a catamaran has much less drag (and weight), combined with a bigger rig for more power and a crew with more leverage to hold that power down.

For these reasons, a catamaran should be a faster and more efficient sailing machine than a dinghy. But all performance is based on compromise and it has to be admitted there are disadvantages with twin-hulled sailing. Catamarans have two hulls, which makes them slightly more expensive to produce than a dinghy. They take up more space, both in the dinghy park due to extra width and on the water due to extra speed. Compared to a dinghy, a catamaran is likely to be more unwieldy to wheel around on a trolley, but that's just a matter of technique. Detractors also accuse catamarans of being slow to tack and having poor ability to sail high into the wind. That may be fair criticism of some older designs, but not of the latest catamarans, which will tack as fast as the crew can manage and point as high as they require.

A catamaran is first and foremost a performance machine – you sail it because you want to go fast and have fun. For this reason, catamaran sailing is perhaps more closely aligned with windsurfing than with traditional dinghy sailing. If the wind is feather-light, the hulls of a catamaran remain stuck to the water and progress is frustratingly slow. A catamaran needs at least Force 2 (see the Beaufort Scale on page 128) to get going and will be at its best in Force 3–5, when it should literally whistle along in any direction. At around Force 4, it should achieve optimum performance. In those conditions a catamaran is easily handled. Everything happens on an extremely stable platform, so it is easy to stop and take a rest. A catamaran can be strongly recommended as an excellent first boat for novices who are just learning to sail, with the proviso that you should beware of potentially fast acceleration and high closing speeds when sharing the water with other boats.

In stronger winds, everything changes, which is to be expected with virtually any boat. If the wind is blowing harder than Force 4, a catamaran will not necessarily go much faster but conditions will certainly become more difficult. Strong winds create waves and load up power in the rig, calling for instant and expert reaction by the crew if they are to stay in control and sail to the maximum. This level of skill comes with experience – lots of practice and time on the water is what counts. ***Enjoy your cat sailing!***

2 | Modern Catamaran Classes

There are many fine catamarans on the water, and the following shown in these pages represent some of the more important milestones in catamaran development.

Shearwater

Shearwater was the first modern catamaran. The class celebrated its 50th birthday in 2006, having been designed by Roland and Francis Prout in 1956, when the original Shearwater created a sailing sensation with its style and speed. Early Shearwaters had an all-wood platform, with a solid centre deck between the two hulls. This was later replaced by the lighter alternative of a mesh trampoline stretched tightly between the hulls and two aluminium beams, an arrangement that has become standard on all modern catamarans.

Shearwater

Steady modifications have allowed the Shearwater to keep pace with the times and maintain an enthusiastic following. The redesigned hulls can now be built in materials such as GRP (glass-reinforced plastic) sandwich for low maintenance, stiffness and light weight, while the sails have a modern plan with a large area of roach supported by full-length battens, built with the latest laminate materials. The Shearwater is virtually unique in having a symmetrical spinnaker, instead of an asymmetric spinnaker, which is fitted to many modern catamarans. It was the first catamaran to have twin trapezes, the first to have a spinnaker and the first to have a spinnaker chute!

Length: 5.09 m; beam 2.28 m; sailing weight 120 kg; mainsail and jib 15.5 sq. m; spinnaker 17.6 sq. m.

A-Class

In 1956 this single-handed catamaran was founded as a free construction class. Due to minimal construction rules to stipulate length, width and sail area it has been possible for designers to develop a boat that remains the fastest of all single-handers. The modern A-Class is a pure high-tech catamaran that is built in carbon or Kevlar, immediately recognisable by a very tall mast with single high-aspect sail. It is the favourite catamaran of some of the world's best racers, who appreciate exceptionally refined performance, but for general use they are possibly too challenging, fragile and expensive!

Length: 5.49 m; beam 2.3 m; sailing weight 75 kg; mainsail 13.94 sq. m.

Tornado

Tornado was the next big development, designed by Rodney March in 1967. The Tornado was characterised by slim hulls that were 20 feet long with a massive 10-foot-wide beam, supporting a large mainsail and jib, which gave it racing performance far superior to any catamaran then available. It was first raced as the Olympic-class catamaran in Canada in 1976, when Reg White and John Osborn won the gold medal. Since then the Tornado has been raced at every Olympic Games, but was updated for the 2004 event in Australia with a bigger rig, an asymmetric spinnaker and twin trapezes, for both crew. The original Tornado, with a smaller mainsail, jib and single trapeze, is now known as the Tornado Classic.

Length: 6.09 m; beam 3.05 m; sailing weight 175 kg; mainsail 18.22 sq. m; jib 5.38 sq. m; asymmetric spinnaker 25.87 sq. m.

A-Class

Tornado

Hobie Cat

Hobie Cat transformed catamaran sailing into a world-wide sport. In 1968 Hobie Alter launched the Hobie 14, designed as a small, fun catamaran that could be launched from any beach, providing a low-cost link between sailboat and surfboard. The single-handed Hobie 14 featured asymmetrical hulls reminiscent of outriggers on a South Pacific proa, with a raised trampoline to clear the waves and a fully battened mainsail to produce sufficient power to sail over them. This concept was so unusual that Hobie Alter had to overcome widespread opposition to his ideas, but he was also a marketing wizard with the determination to succeed. The Hobie 14 was a big success, but it was the double-handed Hobie 16, launched in 1971, that became the best-selling catamaran of all time, with over 100,000 boats sold in three decades. The Hobie 16 is also the world's third-biggest-selling sailboat, only beaten by the Sunfish and the Laser. Fitted with an asymmetric spinnaker for youth racing it is known as the Hobie 16 Spi.

Length: 5.11 m; beam 2.41 m; sailing weight 145 kg; mainsail 13.77 sq. m; jib 5.12 sq m; optional spinnaker 17.5 sq m.

Dart 18 & Sprint 15

Having designed the Tornado as a racing machine for the top league, Rodney March created the Dart 18 in 1976 as a much more practical alternative for everyday sailors. Innovative features include moulded skegs on the hulls for simple handling, beams that slot into the hulls for quick assembly, no boom to spare the crew the pain of getting hit on the head, and a rigid one-design formula to ensure all boats are equally competitive. The Dart 18 has flourished for racing and recreation, with only minor updates to the specification in its first thirty years. In 1978 Rodney March scaled down the Dart 18 design to produce the Sprint 15 (originally known as the Spark). Sprint 15 is one of the few boats that can be sailed with or without a crew on the same handicap and is the biggest single-handed catamaran class in the UK. Unusually for a catamaran, it is car-toppable.

Dart 18: length: 5.48 m; beam 2.28 m; sailing weight 130 kg; mainsail 12.92 sq. m; jib 3.16 sq. m; optional asymmetric spinnaker 17.4 sq. m.

Sprint 15: length: 4.54 m; beam 2.13 m; sailing weight 104 kg; mainsail 10.19 sq. m; jib 2.7 sq. m.

Hobie Cat

Sprint 15

Formula 18

Formula 18 was launched in 1994 as a restricted-design class for twin-trapeze, 18-foot catamarans with an identical SCHRS (Small Cat Handicap Rating System based on measurements) handicap of 1.01. It allows different designs to compete on an equal basis, with two different sail sizes for jib and spinnaker linked to the use of corrector weights to provide fair racing for crews in three weight ranges from 115 to over 150 kg. Materials such as carbon fibre are prohibited to keep costs down. Formula 18 has become established as the top choice for international racing, at both amateur and professional level. The most successful Formula 18 catamaran has been the Hobie Tiger (built in France), which has raced with the class from the start and stages its own Tiger-class European and World championships. Other top performers in Formula 18 include the Nacra (USA), Cirrus (France) and Capricorn (Australia), with at least a dozen more designs to choose from.

Length: 5.52 m; beam 2.6 m; sailing weight 180 kg; mainsail 17 sq. m; jib 3.85 or 4.15 sq. m; asymmetric spinnaker 19 or 21 sq. m.

Formula 18

Hurricane 5.9

Designed by Reg White in 1987 as a more practical alternative to the Tornado. It had similar slim hulls, with the beam reduced so it could be legally towed on roads in most countries – unlike the 10-foot-wide Tornado, which has to be towed at an angle or disassembled. Less beam meant less leverage for the crew to hold down the power in the rig, but this was overcome by fitting twin trapezes, which helped make the shorter and much cheaper one-design Hurricane almost as fast as the classic Tornado. A Hurricane 5.9 SX option is available with spinnaker and modified rig.

Length: 5.9 m; beam 2.43 m; sailing weight 180 kg; mainsail 17.5 sq. m; jib 4.5 sq. m; optional asymmetric spinnaker 21 sq. m.

Hurricane 5.9SX

Having both won gold medals in the Tornado class at the Olympic Games, Yves Loday and Reg White formed a design-and-development partnership to create new catamarans.

Dart 16

Dart 16 was launched in 1997 as a low-cost recreational package, with tough thermoplastic hulls and user-friendly performance.

Length: 4.8 m; beam 2.3 m; sailing weight 150 kg; mainsail 10.4 sq. m; jib 2.7 sq. m; optional asymmetric spinnaker 12 sq. m.

Spitfire

Spitfire, with a twin trapeze, followed in 2000, a pure racing machine for lighter-weight crews, which has excellent tactical performance with the ability to tack as fast as many dinghies.

Length: 5 m; beam 2.53 m; sailing weight 160 kg; mainsail 15.5 sq. m; jib 4.5 sq. m; asymmetric spinnaker 18 sq. m.

Dart 16

Spitfire

Shadow

Shadow followed in 2001, combining very light weight with Kevlar-reinforced hulls for durability. It provides a simple and practical solution to high-performance, single-handed catamaran sailing, with mainsail and a small spinnaker that sets inside the forestay and therefore does not require a pole.

Length: 4.8 m; beam 2.4 m; sailing weight 99 kg; mainsail 13 sq. m; asymmetric spinnaker 10 sq. m.

SL16

Launched in 2003, is based on an older design by Yves Loday. It has been chosen by ISAF as an alternative catamaran class to the Hobie 16 Spi for the annual Youth World Championship, raced by one team from each competing nation up to the age of eighteen. The SL16 is raced with twin trapezes and an asymmetric spinnaker, combining durability with good performance for teenage crews.

Length: 4.8 m; beam 2.32 m; sailing weight 145 kg; mainsail 13.75 sq. m; jib 3.75 sq. m; asymmetric spinnaker 17 sq. m.

Shadow

SL16

VX40

VX40 is the ultimate high-performance catamaran – twice as long and wide as a Tornado, with a wing mast 18.9 metres (62 ft) tall. It was conceived by the top Tornado team of Mitch Booth and Herbert Dercksen, designed by Yves Loday and launched in 2005. Construction is all carbon fibre, built to the highest standards possible by Marstrom in Sweden, which produces the majority of Olympic Tornados. The VX40 is a short-course, inshore racing machine with room for four professional crew and one passenger, who may be the sponsor paying the bill! This extreme one-design class staged its first event at the start of the 2005 Volvo Ocean Race, as a prelude to a Grand Prix series around the world. With a two-part mast, it all fits neatly inside a 40 foot container for transportation.

Length: 12.19 m; beam 7 m; sailing weight 1,307 kg; mainsail 75 sq. m; jib 25 sq. m; reacher 78 sq. m.

VX40

Formula 18 sailors enjoy a high flying ride in waves off Highcliffe in the South of England

3 | What are Catamarans made of?

Plastic Fantastic

'Thermoplastic' rotomoulded polyethylene is used to produce hulls that are low-cost and durable, as found on catamarans such as the Hobie Twixxy and Catsy or Dart 16. Granules of plastic are heated inside a mould, which rotates until the inside is coated with a specific thickness of polyethylene, creating a complete hull with no seams. Hulls can be moulded quickly with minimal labour costs, although initial tooling is expensive. The main compromise with this material is lack of rigidity and extra weight. If a hull flexes, it drains energy and reduces speed through the water, making thermoplastic catamarans better suited to recreational fun than serious racing.

Cats need to be extremely tough for all-round use – the Hobie 16 built in GRP sandwich is about as tough as they come.

Sandwich Solutions

GRP (glass-reinforced plastic) with a lightweight PVC or polyurethane core is the standard hull material for most performance catamarans, often referred to as 'foam-sandwich' construction. The GRP gives the hull strength and resistance to knocks, while the foam core provides overall stiffness with very light weight.

This building system requires female moulds for each complete hull. Older designs such as the Hobie 16 have a separate mould for hull and deck, while more modern designs such as the Hobie Tiger require a mould for the deck plus two moulds for the hull, which is split down the centreline. This gives the builder better access to the entire surface of the mould.

To start the moulding process, a gel coat which will become the shiny outer skin of the hull is either brushed or sprayed onto the inside of a waxed mould. A layer of glass fibre cloth is laid into the mould impregnated with resin, which may be polyester, which is comparatively cheap and easy to work with, or vinylester or epoxy (not allowed in Formula 18). This layer is covered by rigid sheets of foam with a closed-cell structure approximately 3 mm thick, to provide the filling in the 'sandwich', then covered in an airtight bag and vacuumed down to the mould's surface to take the shape of the hull. Extra reinforcement is placed in specific high-stress areas, together with backing pads for the attachment of fittings. The process is completed by an inner layer of glass fibre impregnated with resin.

The finished laminate is left to cure, with the resin transforming it into a solid mass. How long this takes will depend on surrounding temperature and moisture content. Hull and deck, or split hull components, are finally lifted out of their moulds to be bonded together in special joining jigs. Rough edges are removed by grinding and polishing the seam, which will be almost invisible if the job is done well.

At the top of the scale

The best possible weight to strength (impact resistance and hull rigidity) ratio is required to achieve small improvements in ultimate performance. Carbon fibre cloth can provide the best mix of rigidity and light weight, while Kevlar cloth can increase the damage resistance of a super-light hull. Both these materials should be used in conjunction with epoxy resin, which will produce a harder, stronger laminate than polyester resin at the same weight, even when used with conventional glass fibre cloth.

The price of these materials has been steadily falling, but they still cost the boatbuilder considerably more than standard materials and require more skilled workmanship. Epoxy resin is extremely sensitive to temperature and must be 'cooked' correctly to achieve a perfect cure. At the most refined level of construction, the hull of a VX40 is made from a sandwich of pre-preg (pre-impregnated with epoxy resin) carbon which is cooked inside an autoclave chamber at controlled temperature, with 2.5 atmospheres of pressure to press the carbon laminate as tightly as possible into the Nomex foam core which has the appearance of a honeycomb. Each hull is 'baked in a bag' inside the split mould, emerging as a carbon sandwich cylinder with no seams.

The Hobie 16 (above) and Tiger (below) being manufactured in France

Foils for all uses

Rudder blades, daggerboards and centreboards are known as 'foils'. For top performance, they should be as light and stiff as possible. For everyday use, they should be durable enough to resist damage when running aground. Low-cost foils are moulded in a hardwearing solid plastic, such as Lexan, which is used for the Hobie Cat range. For competition use, foam-filled fibreglass with an outer gelcoat creates lighter foils that can be stiffened with carbon string reinforcement. At the top of the scale, the stiffest and lightest foils can be made in wood laminate with clear epoxy outer skin, or foam with a thin layer of carbon fibre and epoxy outer skin.

Beams, booms, masts and spinnaker poles

This is a straight choice between aluminium and carbon fibre. Cost dictates that aluminium is the popular choice, with carbon fibre providing maximum rigidity and light weight. A very few high-performance catamarans, such as A-Class or the VX40 have carbon everything – hulls, foils, beams, booms, masts, poles, tiller bars and extensions. Other classes, such as the Tornado have recently changed from aluminium to carbon masts for lighter weight. However, aluminium masts can be made almost as light by careful engineering of wall thickness, which is increased or reduced in specific areas to produce the required amount of strength and flex. Aluminium masts also have proven performance over many years, while carbon is affected by UV and can suffer unexpected failure.

Basilica

A fun ride in Rio for the crew on the carbon fibre VX40 'Basilica.' As it happens, letting a cat tip this high just slows it down

4 | Choosing a Cat

How much will it cost?

The cost of a catamaran is directly related to materials and components. Catamarans with thermoplastic hulls are likely to have fittings and accessories that enable the manufacturers to provide great value for entry-level and recreational sailing. Catamarans with foam-sandwich construction cover a much wider price range. This is particularly affected by specification. Racing catamarans, such as Formula 18, have the most sophisticated rig possible, which is why their price is considerably higher than recreational catamarans, which require simpler performance. Then there is a huge jump in price up to the Tornado, which has expensive rig and components, uses the best materials and is extremely labour-intensive, as builders strive for perfection. But it's difficult to justify a Tornado costing more than twice as much as a race-ready Formula 18! At the cheapest end of the scale, a good second-hand beach catamaran such as a Dart 18 or Hobie 16 can be bought at very low cost and provide excellent value.

Recreation or race?

It should be possible to enjoy both recreational sailing and racing in any catamaran, but there seems little point paying the extra cost of a dedicated regatta catamaran such as a Tornado or Formula 18 if you don't wish to race. In addition, a high-performance regatta catamaran will be far more demanding on technique.

Performance

All catamarans are fast, but some are faster and more demanding than others. At entry level, it is important to sail a catamaran that is user-friendly and ready to forgive your mistakes. When you have mastered your first catamaran is the time to move to the next level of expertise and performance.

Right: The Hobie 16 is the world's most popular cat – cheap, very tough and equally suitable for beach fun or racing.
Below: A mass of race cats launch during the annual Eurocat event at Carnac in north-west France, with a Tornado and Formula 18 in the foreground.

Durability

All catamarans need to be tough, but some are tougher than others! Thermoplastic and glass fibre are resilient to running aground and general misuse, with heavier catamarans tending to score best on impact-resistance and durability. Materials such as Kevlar may be used to make lightweight catamarans more durable, but they are also more expensive. Foils suffer from misuse, which generally means running aground at speed, scratching or damaging the tips of the foils. Moulded plastic foils are likely to have the best resistance, which makes them the top choice for recreational sailing. Racing foils are not only considerably more expensive, but also more fragile. Their strength lies mainly in their rigidity.

Who will crew?

Most catamarans are twin-crew boats, which means you need someone to sail with on a regular basis. Weight is also an issue. Unless there is a very strong wind, a catamaran will not go fast if its crew are too heavy! In simple terms, two 'heavy weight crew' need a bigger catamaran with longer hulls and more volume to support their weight, plus more sail area to drive them.

Single-handed catamarans avoid the problem of finding a crew and can provide exceptional performance. The top choices include A-Class for the most refined catamaran sailing sensation possible; the Hobie FX1, Inter 17, Shadow or Stealth, which can all provide the challenge of an asymmetric spinnaker; and the traditional Sprint 15, which can be raced with one or two crew.

The FX One provides dedicated single-handed sailing.

Which sails?

Spinnakers are a comparatively recent innovation for catamarans. The asymmetric spinnaker or 'gennaker' started to appear around 1990 and can now be used on most catamarans, either as an optional extra or as a standard fitting on racing boats such as the Spitfire or Formula 18. The advantage of an asymmetric spinnaker is that it provides more interest for the crew and better performance when sailing downwind. Disadvantages are additional cost and complexity for the catamaran, and you have to learn spinnaker techniques.

Skegs or boards?

All sailing boats make leeway, which means that they drift sideways instead of going straight ahead. A centreboard or a daggerboard provides a flat foil that combats this sideslip. Alternatively, the Hobie 16 has asymmetric hulls that are flat on the outside to combat sideslip. Nacra pioneered the skeg, which is like a keel incorporated into the moulding of each hull. Skegs are now standard on the majority of recreational catamarans, but do not allow a catamaran to point as high upwind or sail as deep downwind as with daggerboards.

A centreboard swivels on a pivot inside its case. A daggerboard moves straight up and down in its case. Either system should provide better performance than a skeg. However, extra complexity and cost are involved when building centreboards or daggerboards into a catamaran. The boards must be operated correctly by the crew, are prone to damage if they hit the bottom, and require maintenance. By contrast, skegs are reasonably efficient, add negligible cost to the boat, require no input from the crew, don't suffer if you run aground, and provide a strong, reinforced bottom when pulling a catamaran up the beach.

"Which cat would you like, sir?"

Sail with a trapeze

A trapeze provides the crew with greater leverage, allowing you to stand out on the side of the boat. The technique is easy and you get a great view! Virtually all catamarans are fitted with a single trapeze. Many catamarans have twin trapezes, for both crew and helm, which require greater expertise. However, you don't have to use the trapeze. No matter how strong the wind, it's always possible to sail a catamaran sitting on the side.

Other costs

You have bought the perfect catamaran! Now add all the possible extra costs of sailing clothes, buoyancy aid, harness, trolley, road trailer, protective covers, dinghy-club membership, and a place in the boat park or launching fees. Sails, control lines, shockcords and fittings may wear out and need to be replaced. Spinnakers are prone to tears, while foils and hulls suffer minor damage, which requires your time with a repair kit. Add the cost of insurance, which is vital at third-party level at least. Deal with a broker that specialises in catamaran insurance and has standard rates for the best-known designs.

The Nacra Infusion is fitted with twin trapezes, asymmetric spinnaker and daggerboards to provide plenty of performance and fun.

Hobie 16s racing in rough conditions at the 2005 World Championship in Port Elizabeth, South Africa.

5 Cat Components and Controls

The Platform

The platform on which the crew sails the boat is composed of hulls, beams and trampoline.

* Beams provide a rigid structure for the catamaran. The rear beam incorporates a full-length mainsheet traveller, so the angle of the mainsail can be changed for sailing downwind. The front beam is often used as a mounting point for jib sheets and spinnaker halyard.

* The front beam supports the rig, with the base of the mast resting on a ball which allows it to rotate. To resist the downward force of the mast, the beam may have a V-shaped dolphin striker fitted on the underside. Alternatively, internal reinforcement and extra wall thickness may be combined with a curved shape to ensure sufficient rigidity.

* The trampoline is made of lightweight, self-draining mesh which is extremely durable – but quite hard on your knees! It is attached to the beams or sides of the hulls using slots or lacing. The trampoline should be tensioned so it is virtually rigid and will not sag with the weight of the crew.

The Storm 20 features an extra-wide platform.

A dolphin striker reinforces the front beam.

The Dart 16 (left) and Hobie Tiger (right) use similar components and controls maximised for recreational and regatta sailing.

The Rotating Wing

From bird wings to catamarans

Catamaran rigs are bigger, more powerful and have considerably more load under acceleration than the rigs on most sailing dinghies. The rig must be extremely stable with an aerodynamic shape that promotes smooth airflow over the mainsail.

Virtually all catamarans use a rotating 'wing' mast with an elliptical section, supporting a mainsail with full-length battens. This concept was developed by Dr Manfred Curry in the 1920s. Dr Curry was a German scientist and dinghy sailor who dissected bird wings to help design his sails. Less contentiously, he subjected his prototypes to wind and smoke tests at the Junkers aircraft factory. Dr Curry discovered it was possible to increase power by using full-length ash battens to provide a rigid and stable sail shape, and this remains true today. He also built 'teardrop' or wing-shaped masts to provide an aerofoil that improves performance by reducing turbulence when wind flows over the sail.

Dr Manfred Curry would appreciate the rotating wing-shape mast and full length battens of a modern cat.

Let the mast rotate

The wing mast of a catamaran is supported by a stainless-steel wire forestay and two shrouds attached to a single point at the front of the mast. (Synthetic line such as Kevlar is a possible lightweight alternative.) The shrouds have a bridle to connect to the two hulls. To allow the mast to rotate, a cup at the base locks onto a ball mounted on the front beam.

There are two good reasons for allowing a wing mast to partially rotate. Firstly, maximum performance can only be achieved if the wing mast is correctly aligned with its fully battened sail. It must rotate if there is a major change in direction, which happens during every tack and gybe, or if there is a change from upwind to downwind sailing (or vice versa) in light winds.

Secondly, reducing or increasing mast rotation can be used to control power from the mainsail. The amount of rotation is controlled by a lever on the mast, called a 'spanner', with a control line that is often led to a cleat on top of the boom. If there is too much wind, adjusting the control line to 'derotate' the mast can depower the sail by interfering with airflow. For maximum power, the mast rotation lever should be pointing at the shrouds, promoting perfect airflow. If the wind is too strong, tightening the control line will rotate the mast towards the back of the boat to increase turbulence and reduce power.

The Controls

Mainsail

- The primary control for the mainsail is the mainsheet, which is so heavily loaded it requires auto-ratchet blocks and pulleys with at least 6:1 power to enable the crew to sheet in as required. The mainsheet should always be tensioned so that both windward and leeward telltales flow smoothly back along the sail.

- The top block of the mainsheet is attached to the end of the boom or clew of the mainsail. The bottom block of the mainsheet is attached to a slider on the main traveller mounted on the rear beam. A traveller control line locks the mainsheet in a fixed position on the traveller. Normal position is as close to the centre as possible upwind, across the wind roughly half way and downwind, three quarters away. In strong winds, letting the bottom mainsheet block slide a short distance down the traveller can reduce mainsail power and help maintain control. In very light winds, a catamaran can sail faster downwind with the bottom mainsheet block near the outer end of the traveller.

- The boom is attached to the mast by a gooseneck, which allows the boom to swivel in a horizontal arc between the shrouds. On modern catamarans, the boom's primary role is to manage tension in the foot of the mainsail. An outhaul control line attached to the clew can be loosened to create a fuller shape with more power for light winds, or tightened for a flatter and more stable shape in stronger winds.

- The downhaul (above and below) is used to tension the luff of the mainsail and compress the mast. Increasing downhaul induces further mast bend which flattens the shape of the mainsail and decreases power. This 'opens' the top of the sail with the head twisting away from the wind. On a racing catamaran the downhaul requires a powerful pulley system for easy operation – for instance the Tornado uses a 16:1 downhaul. Control lines can be led to either side of the boat so the crew can adjust tension while out on the trapeze. Downhaul tension should be eased off for sailing downwind.

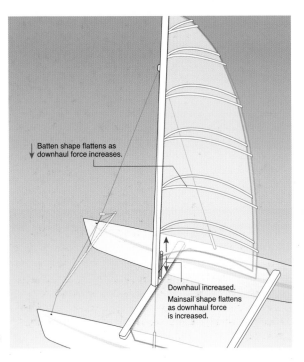

Batten shape flattens as downhaul force increases.

Downhaul increased.
Mainsail shape flattens as downhaul force is increased.

Jib

- Many modern catamarans have the jib mounted on a furler, which makes management almost fail-safe. You pull a control line and the jib rolls up when it's not needed! A conventional jib system has jib sheets led through jamming cleats on the port and starboard side of the forward beam. A more refined alternative is the self-tacking jib. This system tacks or gybes automatically, sliding along a curved track mounted on the forward beam. A single sheet controls fullness and sail angle.

- Getting the jib correctly aligned with the mainsail is critical for promoting the 'slot effect', which accelerates airflow over the leeward side of the mainsail and maximises performance.

- Jib performance can also be enhanced by using a luff downhaul system to reduce power. Some jibs have a triple sheeting position on the clew. Middle position is standard. Bottom position tightens the foot and loosens the leech, to reduce power in stronger winds. Top position loosens the foot and tightens the leech, to increase power in lighter winds.

Spinnaker

Asymmetric spinnakers are standard on many modern catamarans – they enhance downwind performance and provide the crew with extra fun in lighter winds. Most catamarans use a spinnaker chute or 'snuffer', mounted between the front beam and bridle, which may be an integral part of the spinnaker pole. The spinnaker is launched from the chute by the crew pulling on the halyard control line, which is a continuous loop. The spinnaker is pulled back inside the chute when the crew pulls this line in the opposite direction for retrieval. A continuous sheet controls the sheeting angle of the spinnaker.

The original system of launching the spinnaker from a bag on the trampoline is obsolete. The chute system removes the clutter of a large bag from the trampoline. Hoisting or dropping the spinnaker is faster and more reliable, with no requirement to drop on the 'right' side of the boat which was another disadvantage of the bag system.

Rudder systems

- Rudder foils must be perfectly aligned so that they are parallel. Each foil must be fully down. If there is any 'weather helm' with the tiller pulling away from you, it generally means the rudder foils are not fully down. The amount of rudder rake relates to mast rake. Mast back requires rudders forward and vice versa.

- Different catamarans have different engineering for the rudder foil and rudder case in which it can swivel from a fully up to fully down position. The main requirement is that the foils must stay rigidly locked in position when down, but will unlock immediately if they hit the bottom and are easy to unlock and lift for coming ashore.

- Each case has a short tiller connected by a long tiller bar. To enable the helm to steer the boat when hiking or trapezing, the tiller bar has a long tiller extension. Telescopic extensions are available for easy handling.

- The cranked tiller arms on most catamarans are based on Ackerman's Arc Theory. This states that the inside hull turns in a tighter circle than the outer hull. Consequently the rudders must operate at different angles to avoid a braking effect, employing a similar concept to front-wheel steering on a car.

The Tornado has centreboards which swivel backwards instead of the more normal daggerboards shown below

Different boards

Apart from the Tornado (above) and Hurricane 5.9, centreboards that swivel up and down inside a case have become rare on catamarans. They are expensive to build into the hulls and, with less vertical area, do not provide as much 'lift' as a daggerboard. On the plus side, centreboards are easy for the crew to operate by pulling or pushing on the handle. They will also swivel back if they hit the bottom, unlike daggerboards, which are likely to damage themselves or their cases.

Daggerboards must be a tight fit with minimum movement for best performance. This can make it difficult for the crew to push them all the way down and even more difficult to pull them up! Beware of sailing at speed with daggerboards half-lifted. If the catamaran takes a nosedive, the crew may be thrown forward against the sharp trailing edge, which is potentially dangerous.

The SL16 uses built-in skegs to prevent leeway, with only rudder blades deep beneath the waterline.

6 | Clothing and Equipment

Catamaran sailing can be cold. Unless you sail where both wind and water are hot, the price you pay for a catamaran's performance is wind-chill. The faster you go, the colder it gets! Wind-chill cuts the immediate temperature around your body on a sliding scale. An air temperature of 10°C is reduced to 8.2°C by an apparent wind of 5 knots, which drops to 0°C if the wind increases to 35 knots. Regardless of the temperature, no one should be sailing a catamaran in Force 7–8!

If you get cold on the water, sailing a catamaran will become unpleasant. It may become dangerous, since hypothermia is ready to threaten the ill-prepared watersports enthusiast. Thankfully, excellent clothing is available to overcome problems with cold in all but the most severe weather.

Cold Conditions

Always wear a drysuit. A good quality drysuit built from breathable material is expensive but very worthwhile. Worn with a synthetic thermal base layer, plus mid-layer if required, it will keep your body warm without too much heat building up inside. A drysuit with latex rubber socks is recommended. Socks are much easier to get on and off than ankle seals, with the bonus of keeping your feet dry. Latex socks are fragile, so never step out in them without boots, and choose a drysuit with ankle cuffs for maximum protection. Latex wrist and neck seals are one size, so they generally have to be trimmed for a perfect fit. Use very sharp scissors and cut carefully round one ring at a time. Remember that the neck seal in particular will stretch in use on the water.

Drysuits have a choice of front or back zips. The back zip feels less bulky, but you can't get out of that zip without a helping hand. So the front zip is the top choice for most people. Wash off salt and store the drysuit on a plastic hanger in a cool, dark environment. Treat seals with a proprietary lubricant at regular intervals. Be aware that latex seals will eventually perish. If a seal fails when you are sailing, it will surely be unpleasant, and could be dangerous, as your drysuit fills with water. Replacing seals before it's too late is an inexpensive and straightforward operation. The drysuit zip needs a regular wash with fresh water. An occasional rub with candle wax will ensure smooth sliding – you can briefly melt the wax into the teeth with a hair dryer.

Drysuits are damaged by overexposure to direct sunlight or heat. Leaving a drysuit on the rear shelf of your car is not recommended.

Talcum powder lets hands slide through seals.

Put in one arm at a time.

Hold the neck seal wide apart.

Stretch the zip as you pull.

Make sure the zip is shut!

Expel all surplus air.

Warm Conditions

It is rare to be able to sail a catamaran comfortably without a wetsuit. Catamaran sailing at speed can be a wet pastime, as the crew are bombarded by spray, which soon makes you cold. Wetsuits are available for all weathers. The thickness of the neoprene used determines their warmth, which also depends on a very close fit with watertight seams and zip to prevent cold water flushing through the suit and lowering your body temperature. Wetsuits for winter use will typically be made of 5 mm neoprene for the body and legs with 3 mm for arms and shoulders, which require extra mobility. For summer use, 3 mm neoprene will suffice and make the suit considerably lighter and more flexible.

When choosing a wetsuit a perfect fit is vital. All wetsuits have a Lycra inner lining to make the neoprene easier to pull on and off your body. This also relies on the stretchiness of the neoprene – a super-stretchy suit will pull on and off like a glove. Make sure you can operate the rear-entry zip unassisted – some zips are easier to pull than others!

It is vital that a wetsuit for catamaran sailing has reinforcement pads on the knees. The trampoline is hard and will wear through unprotected neoprene. For this reason, it's not a great idea to sail a catamaran with a shortie wetsuit and bare knees!

The principal advantages of a wetsuit over a drysuit are lower cost, less bulk and less chance of overheating. If a wetsuit feels cold in marginal conditions, wearing a windproof spraytop should solve the problem. You may also like to wear a nylon rash vest underneath, which protects bare skin from rubbing against the seams of a wetsuit and can provide extra insulation.

A good quality wetsuit will last for many years with basic maintenance. Always wash the wetsuit in fresh water after saltwater use, ensuring salt does not build up in the zip. Allow the suit to dry and store in a cool, dark place on a plastic hanger. Do not leave the suit folded or crumpled, and keep it out of direct sunlight. Small tears in the neoprene can be repaired with super-glue. Since the wetsuit is worn next to your body, personal hygiene is important – a maltreated wetsuit can become a highly unpleasant bacteria-ridden garment.

If the wind is up you need full wetsuit protection, however warm the weather is back on dry land.

6   Clothing and Equipment

Hands and Feet

You need dedicated sailing gloves to handle the narrow-diameter, synthetic control lines and high sheet loads of a catamaran. Gloves suitable for most three-season conditions typically have reinforced synthetic-leather palms for excellent grip, lightweight mesh backs for quick draining, Velcro wrist-straps for precise fit and short fingers for picking out lines.

It's pleasant to sail a catamaran barefoot, but boots will provide better grip and protect your feet against bashes. The best choice is neoprene boots that cover your ankles and have a zip, combining thermal insulation, protection and an easy fit. The soles should grip like limpets on the side of the boat and not 'roll' on your feet – this can be prevented by Velcro straps to tension the uppers. Kneeling on the side of a catamaran also puts a lot of stress on the uppers. This tends to destroy lightweight sailing shoes and makes a tough pair of boots the best option.

Staying afloat

A buoyancy aid is designed to provide sufficient (50 Newton) buoyancy to float a fully conscious person. It should not be confused with a lifejacket, which is designed to turn an unconscious person face-up in the water, but is impractical for catamaran sailing.

A vest-style buoyancy aid is lightweight and compact, providing maximum freedom of movement on the boat or in the water. It should be worn as your outer garment. If worn with a trapeze harness, the buoyancy aid must be high enough not to obstruct the hook. A buoyancy aid also provides useful thermal insulation and protection against knocks.

Hooking on

Using a trapeze has progressed to standard practice, with many modern catamarans fitted with twin trapeze wires for helm and crew. The standard harness for catamaran sailing has a stainless-steel bar to spread the load of the hook, mounted on a well-padded 'nappy'-style seat with reinforcement to support the lower back and adjustable straps for a tight fit around the hips. Most harnesses have shoulder straps to support the upper body. On a harness such as the Hobie Convertible, these straps can be removed for maximum upper-body mobility.

An alternative to the standard trapeze hook is the Bethwaite 'No Hook' trapeze system. This features a composite trapeze buckle on the harness that slots into a ball on the end of each trapeze wire. The first advantage is that there is no hook to catch on lines or rigging; a possible danger in a capsize. The second advantage is that there is no hook to scratch the boat as you climb onto the side. The principal disadvantage is that the ball is less secure than a hook when racing.

Dress for the conditions and make sure all your clothing and equipment is functional.

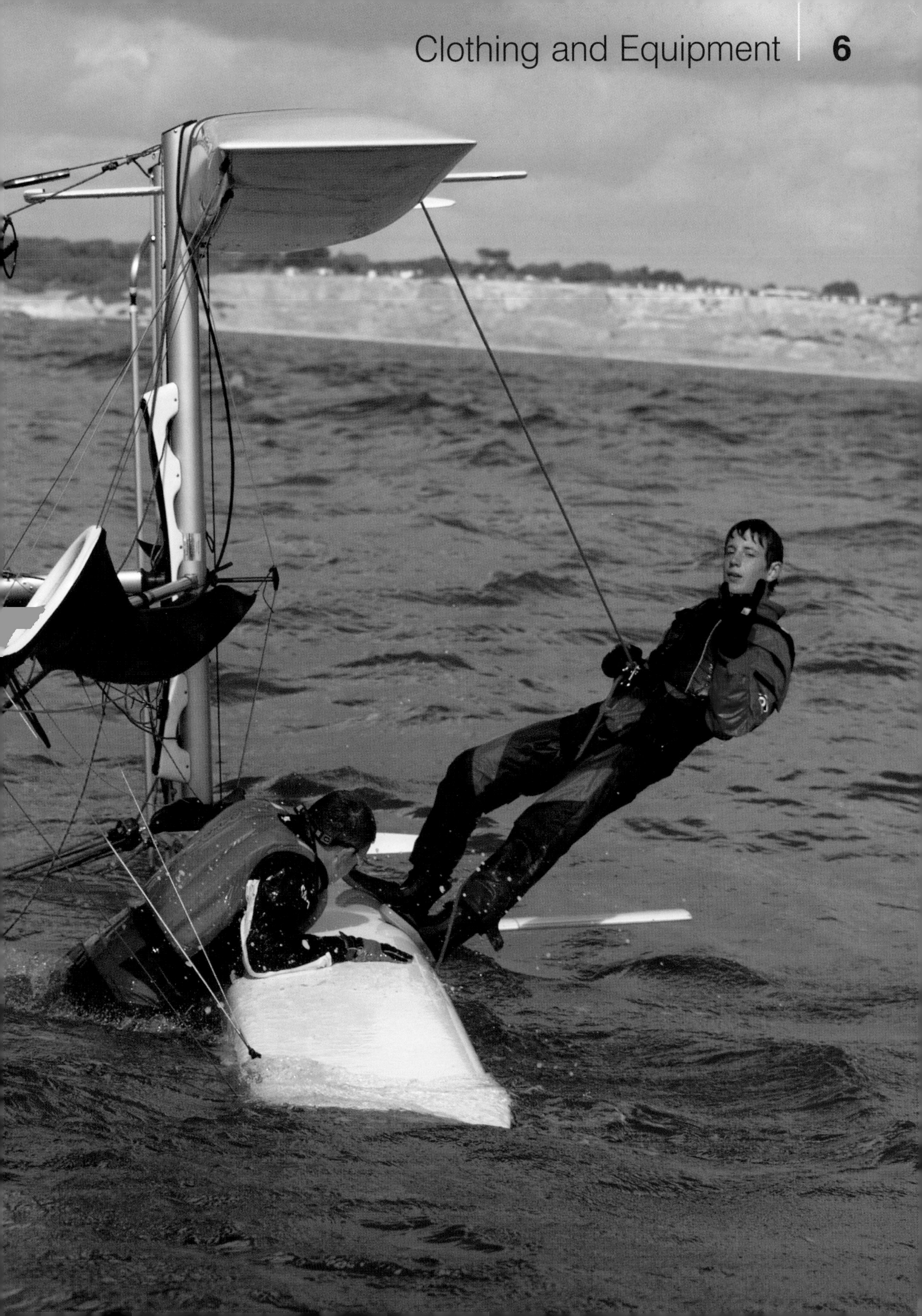

7 Building a Platform

Most cat sailors never assemble or disassemble their platform. A new cat is invariably supplied ready-to-sail, which leaves the experts to build the platform. A cat should only require disassembly under certain situations:

- Your cat is being shipped abroad in a container.

- You don't have much space for winter storage – it's easier with separate hulls and beams.

- You enjoy the whole business of disassembly which can be used as an annual maintenance check.

- You sail a Tornado which is wider than the legal towing limit. Hulls, beams and trampoline must be taken apart every time you travel to a regatta. (It is legal to tow a complete Tornado on a special tilting trailer.)

Putting it together

Building a cat platform has many variations which will be explained in manuals for individual designs. A new Hobie 15 is being built on these pages, but the principles of attaching hulls, beams and trampoline are similar for all cats. Two people and at least a couple of hours will be required for this operation.

Choose a neat, uncluttered area where you can lay out the hulls, beams and all components on the plastic wrapping. Be careful if you do this on the beach. It's easy to lose small bits of boat in the sand and you don't want sand or dirt getting inside holes and slots.

Position the hulls parallel on the ground approximately 2 metres apart. Prepare the crossbeams which will be attached to the hulls with one or two heavy duty nuts and bolts on each end of the beam.

Attach the front beam to one hull, which may be easier with the hull held upright or sideways as shown. Screw the bolts hand tight. Then attach the other front hull to the front beam. Finally, attach the rear beam both sides and increase torque on the bolts.

That was the easy bit! Attaching the mesh trampoline and getting it as taut as possible takes effort, patience and time. Most modern cat trampolines use bolt ropes fed along grooves in the beams or hulls combined with lace tensioning at the corners, down the middle or along the sides. The trick is to lace everything up evenly and then apply sufficient tension to transform mesh cloth into an almost rigid deck.

Disassembly follows the reverse procedure. Beware that a cat platform which has been left assembled on the beach for several years may be surprisingly difficult to pull apart!

Lay out and check all the components in a clear working area where everything comes to hand. Don't lose bits on the beach!

Attach front and rear beams to the hulls to form the main platform. Bolts must be carefully aligned and tightened.

The webbing belt slides into the front beam, with the two halves of the trampoline sliding into the rear beam and sides.

Lacing and tensioning the trampoline until it is as rigid as possible requires care and patience.

8 | Trailing a Catamaran

Trailing a catamaran

On the road

- Maximum legal width for trailing is 2.6 metres (8 feet) on most European roads. The majority of catamarans can be towed fully assembled, with the exception of the Tornado, which is 3.05 metres (10 feet) wide.

- The maximum speed limit when trailing on UK roads is 60 mph. Different countries have different speed limits and trailer restrictions.

- A functional lighting board and reflective number plate must be attached to the back of the boat. The foot of the mast should not protrude beyond the sterns.

Choosing a trailer

Catamaran trailers are purpose-built. Two-wheel trailers are adequate for catamarans up to 20 feet. A separate braking system is not required for a relatively light load of less than 300 kg including the trailer. Features should include:

- Rollers at the correct width to support both hulls.

- A large, lockable trailer box with all the space you need for sails, spares, tools, drysuits and wetsuits.

- A jockey wheel that can be wound down for pushing the trailer around a boat park. A common mistake is to leave the jockey wheel down when towing – don't do it.

- A spare wheel in case of punctures or bearing failure, plus a tool to remove wheel-nuts.

Packing a trailer

- Develop a system that works for you, when packing or unpacking a trailer. Make sure everything is secure and will not come loose with movement or vibration. Make sure nothing will rub and cause damage.

- The hulls should be firmly strapped down onto the trailer. Beware of straps cutting through the deck – small pieces of carpet can be used to provide a protective barrier. Be very careful when using narrow-diameter rope to tie things down.

- Pull the forestay, shrouds and trapeze wires tight, roll them tightly around the mast and secure with tape. Make sure the mast is tied down at the front crutch and on the back beam. Black anodising on masts and beams can get scratched. Use padding under the mast where it rests on the rear beam.

- Foils are vulnerable to damage. Daggerboards and rudders should be packed in foil bags and transported inside the trailer box.

- Before going on a long trip, check tyre pressure and tread.

Roof-rack catamarans

Some smaller catamarans, such as the Sprint 15, are car-toppable. The hulls can be transported upside-down on a car roof rack, with enough space for the beams and a two-part mast. This is a useful feature for sailors who tow a caravan.

Trailer sense

- On the first few attempts at trailing, make regular stops to check the trailer and its load.

- Be aware that the catamaran you are towing will probably be wider than your car.

- Roads are dirty. Hull-covers ensure you will not arrive with a filthy boat.

- Keep the trailer out of salt water! Always use the trolley to launch and recover your catamaran.

Opposite; A trailer box is vital for carrying sails and gear
Above; The jockey wheel allows you to raise the front of the trailer
Below; Double check everything is secure before you drive away

9 | Rigging a Catamaran

Rigging a catamaran has many variations, but the principles remain the same.

Raising the mast

Raising or lowering the mast is considerably easier with two people.

- Before you start, beware of overhead power lines, trees and other obstructions.
- If there is a breeze, turn the boat so that the stern points into the wind.
- Lay the mast on top of the two beams with the base at the front of the boat.
- Attach the end of the two shrouds to the shroud-plates on the hulls. Push in the clevis pins at the correct position on one side and the top hole, loosest position on the other side. Secure with split rings, which can be a fiddle in cold weather.
- Ensure the forestay has no tangles.
- Remove the security bolt from the mast base. Rigger No.1 holds the head of the mast. Rigger No.2 places the cup in the base of the mast on the mast step ball, and then refits the security bolt to the mast base with a nut for added safety.
- Rigger No.1 walks forward, pushing the mast up hand-over-hand, until he can stand on the trampoline. Rigger No.2 gives a helping hand by pulling on the forestay. Alternatively, rigger 1 walks the mast to the back of the tramp and then hands it to rigger 2 who gets up onto the tramp to take over the mast as rigger 1 goes forward to attach the forestay.

Mast base attached to the mast step ball.

Walk the mast up and attach forestay.

- When the mast is upright, rigger no.2 connects the end of the forestay to the shroud-plate on the bridle wire linked to both bows. Choose an upper hole for reasonable mast rake.

- With forestay and shrouds secure, remove the security bolt from the mast base to allow unrestricted rotation.

- Tension the port and starboard shrouds. The rigging should feel firm to the hand all round. A good method is for rigger no.1 to haul back on a trapeze wire, allowing rigger no.2 to take up the slack and move the shroud to a lower position on its plate. Alternatively, if there is no wind you can hoist the mainsail. Pull the mainsheet down on one side of the traveller so that the shroud is slack enough for adjustment. Then repeat on the other side.

Pull on tension to attach the shrouds.

Attaching the forestay – don't drop the pin or ring!

Trapeze wires

Each trapeze wire is attached to a trapeze ring (or Bethwaite system ball) by an adjustable-length control line. Each control line is attached to a shockcord to keep the trapeze wire under tension when not in use. The shockcord is generally secured under the trampoline or along the front beam, connected to the control line with a double bowline (shown below right). The simplest way to tie the control line to the trapeze handle is an 'Australian bowline' – one overhand knot in the end of the line and one overhand knot round the handle (shown below left).

The Catsailors' useful knot guide

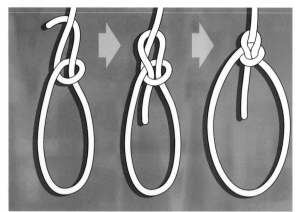

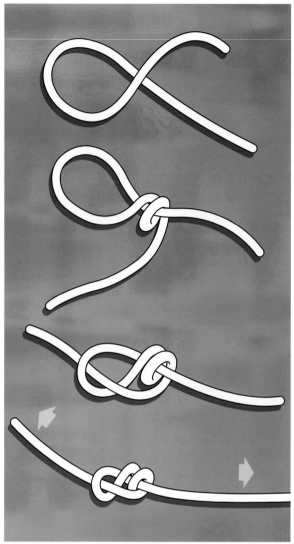

Bowline: attaching jib sheets to blocks, trapeze elastics, two loops.

Figure-of-eight: mainsheet traveller stopper knot.

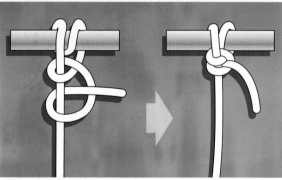

Round turn and two half hitches: mooring to a post or buoy.

Double figure-of-eight: attaching spinnaker tack; securing head and top patch of spinnaker.

Flat out fun – not the best time for any knot to come undone…

Rudder assembly

- Identify the port and starboard rudders. The rudder is attached to the hull with heavy-duty stainless-steel pins known as 'pintles'. The simplest rudder designs, as used on most sailing dinghies, drop on and lock.

- Some rudder designs are more complex. Catamarans in the Hobie range have a single full-length pintle secured with split rings. This is extremely secure and rigid, but fiddly to get into place. It can be difficult to dismantle if the rudders have been on the back of the boat for a long period.

- A transverse tiller bar locates on top of the tillers. Each end of the tiller bar may drop onto a pin with a security catch, which is the simplest system; or be attached with bolt, nut and nylon washers to allow easy movement from side to side.

- The tiller extension is attached to the middle of the tiller crossbar using a clevis pin and split ring.

Inserting the full length pin is fiddly, but provides an extremely rigid rudder attachment on the transons.

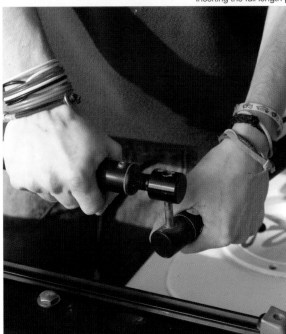

The tiller bar is attached to each tiller, with the extension attached in the middle of the tiller bar.

Setting the rudders

The rudders must be aligned. The simplest method (as shown below) is to look along the hull and ensure that the starboard rudder blade points down the centreline, and then check the angle of the port rudder blade. This can be adjusted by lengthening or shortening the tiller bar. The standard setting is both rudder blades parallel, which gives a neutral feel to the tiller. Some catamaran sailors prefer blades slightly 'toed in' (long tiller bar) to give slight 'weather helm' – the tiller pulls, so the catamaran turns towards the wind unless corrected.

TAPE IT UP! Clevis pins and split rings have two nasty habits. Firstly, they can come undone. Secondly, they can catch on your clothing or the spinnaker and have a ripping time. To ensure this never happens, always cover pins and rings with insulating tape. (Roll it on so that the plastic shroud covers will slide over easily.) Check around the boat for bits sticking out and sharp edges. If in doubt, tape them up.

Hoisting Sails

Mainsail

Before you start, ensure the boat is pointing into the wind.

- The mainsail of a catamaran is rolled around its full-length battens, for simple storage without putting creases in the sail. When not in use, the battens should be loosened. When you go sailing, pull on enough batten tension to take up the curved shape of the sail and remove any wrinkles.

- Unroll the sail on the trampoline with the bolt rope at the front. Feed the head of the sail into the cut-out in the mast track.

- Loosen the main halyard. Attach the shackle to the headboard of the sail.

- Pull on the main halyard while feeding the mainsail bolt rope into the mast track. On some catamarans it can be a tight fit. You may need rigger no.1 to pull the halyard and rigger no.2 to feed the sail.

- With no luff tension (downhaul), the mainsail will stay fairly quiet with the boat pointing into wind. Always let downhaul right off when you leave a catamaran at rest.

F18 headboard lock.

Feeding the mainsail.

Pulling on downhaul.

Inserting bottom of the luff.

Attaching the clew to the boom.

Halyard locks

• Due to heavy loads, virtually all catamarans have a halyard lock at the top of the mast, which prevents the halyard stretching when the mainsail is fully powered. Most catamarans have a short wire strop between the rope halyard and the head of the sail. The end of the wire strop has a ferrule or stopper that locks against a V-shape fitting on the front of the mast.

• On bright sunny days this operation can require sunglasses for gazing at the top of the mast! Haul the sail up to the top of the mast, lining up the wire halyard in the jaws of the 'V' with the stopper approximately 5 mm beneath. Then ease down the halyard so that the stopper pulls hard against the 'V' when the sail drops down.

• Reverse the procedure to drop the mainsail. Pull down hard on the halyard, lift the stopper clear of the jaws and drop the sail. Sometimes this is easier said than done.

• High-performance catamarans, such as Formula 18, have a slightly different system, with the headboard at the top of the sail locking directly to the mast head.

Halyard lock on the Hobie 15 is just below the mast float

• Secure the loose end of the main halyard on the cleat at the base of the mast. Tuck any excess into a pocket on the trampoline, but do not mix it with the righting line.

Luff tension

Downhaul is used to tension the luff and power up the mainsail. Attach the top block of the downhaul system to the tack of the sail. Ensure the bottom of the bolt rope is fed into the lower part of the mast track, before pulling on slight tension. Do not pull on full tension until you are ready to begin sailing.

Mainsheet and traveller control

- Thread the tail of the mainsheet through the jamming cleat and fairlead on the rear crossbar then through the main traveller car and down through the central padeye fitting at the back of the crossbeam, where it can be secured by a figure-of-eight knot. This is your traveller control line.

- There should be no crossovers or twists in a properly threaded system. Attach the mainsheet ratchet block to the top of the main traveller using a clevis pin and split ring or shackle. Lay the sheet and top block on the trampoline, ready to hook onto the clew of the sail when you launch the boat.

Make sure the mainsheet is not twisted, thread the tail through jamming cleat, fairlead & traveller car on the rear crossbeam, secured by a figure of eight

Attach the mainsheet ratchet block to the top of the main traveller. Remember to tape up the clevis pin or tighten the shackle

  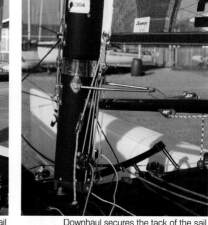

The top block of the mainsheet is connected to the clew of the sail

Downhaul secures the tack of the sail

Jib attachment

- Most catamarans are fitted with a furler, which is convenient for rolling up the jib while sailing or on dry land. The rolled jib should be derigged when the catamaran is not in use for long periods, to avoid degradation from sunlight. Otherwise a jib cover is recommended. These can be made by a local sail repairer.

- The jib is raised by a halyard attached by a shackle to the head. The tack is attached to the top of the furler with a shackle. Most catamarans use full-length zippers to attach the luff around the forestay, as an alternative to the traditional clips or hanks on the Dart 18 and Sprint 15.

- On some boats (Hobie 16) the end of the halyard can be cleated to the mast, with excess line stowed in a bag. Others have a long halyard to hoist the jib, called a 'lazy' halyard, which is then removed and stowed. Then a short 'working ' halyard is used to tension the jib luff, leaving much less rope to stow away. Luff tension is provided by a pulley system at the tack of the sail. On some catamarans, such as the Dart 16, the halyard locks into a cleat at the top of the sail with a pulley for luff tension.

- Because of high loads, the jib will normally be fitted with two small jib-clew blocks, providing a double purchase with jib-sheet blocks mounted on the port and starboard sides of the front beam. A continuous jib sheet is threaded through the sheet blocks and round the clew blocks. Each end is tied to the top of a sheet block using a bowline.

- The jib is rolled by pulling on the thin furling line led through a small jamming cleat on the front beam. To unroll the sail, unjam the furling line and pull on either jib sheet.

Zipper jibs

High-performance catamarans have a full-length zip to attach the jib luff around the forestay with a more aerodynamic shape. A line is used to pull the wire halyard down inside the sleeve as the jib goes up and the zip comes down. The end of the wire is secured to the jib-luff tensioner at the base of the sail, with the line normally removed for sailing. Some catamarans have an adjustable jib downhaul with a control line led back to the main beam.

Start from the top of the zip.

Zip down and pull up.

The tack is attached to the chain plate.

A pulley provides final luff tension.

Securing the halyard on the tack cleat.

Self-tacking jibs

A self-tacking jib has a single clew block, with the single sheet led through a sliding block on the traveller and back to a jamming cleat. A control line restricts how far the main block can slide from side to side.

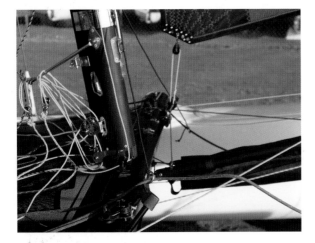

Righting line

A righting line is used to pull the catamaran back upright after a capsize – don't sail without it. The righting line is a thick, soft rope with two or three granny knots for better grip. It can be secured to the dolphin striker, front beam or mast base with the free end of the line coiled inside a transom pocket that should be reserved exclusively for this use.

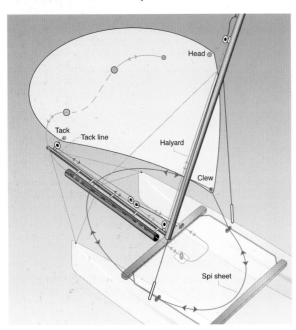

Remember the plugs!

Each hull has a drain plug, which must be screwed tight. When not sailing, the plugs should be removed to drain any water inside and allow the hulls to breathe. Also check that inspection hatches are tightly closed before you go sailing.

Spinnaker

- The spinnaker snuffer system is standard with many catamarans and can be retro-fitted to most older designs. The spinnaker is stored inside a chute attached to the spinnaker pole. The main body of the chute is tough cloth or a hard laminate material. The mouth of the chute requires a hard ring (stainless-steel or plastic) or moulded section, like the mouth of a trumpet, to let the spinnaker slide freely in and out.

- A continuous halyard passes through the chute. It is attached to the head of the spinnaker for hoisting (pulling the line towards the back of the boat) and to the body of the spinnaker so that it can be retrieved (pulling the line towards the front of the boat) in a controlled bundle that does not fall into the water. Most spinnakers have holes or patches for the downhaul line. The line passes in and out through the holes and is secured with a figure-of-eight.

- A continuous single sheet is led through ratchet blocks and routed round the outside of the forestay, with both ends attached to the clew of the sail.

- Some high-performance catamarans have a separate outhaul control line, which pulls the spinnaker out to the end of the pole before the hoist. This allows a faster hoist, since the spinnaker is not being pulled back against the mouth of the chute.

Spinnaker sense

- Use a double figure-of-eight for attaching each sheet to the clew of the spinnaker. The sheet that wraps round the forestay must be passed behind the head and halyard before being attached to its clew.

- It's vital to ensure the spinnaker will go up without tangles. Check down both sides and along the foot to make sure the spinnaker is not twisted before attaching lines. Hoist the spinnaker on dry land for a final check.

1. Attach head.
2. Run hand down port side of spi to tack of sail.
3. Attach tackline.
4. Find foot of sail. Then guide spi halyard through spi patches or rings from foot to head of sail.
5. Put stopper knot in spi halyard after final patch near head of sail.
6/7/8. Hoist spi to check all is correct and no lines crossed.
9. Drop spi.
10/11/12. Attach port and starboard spi sheets.
13. Hoist again and check that sheets don't go around front of spi.
14. Drop and retrieve into trumpet to check all is correct.

At the end of the day

- Derigging is a reverse procedure.

- If you sail on salt water, wash everything down with a hose when possible to prevent build-up of salt crystals, which can cut into sail material and corrode fittings. Allow the sails to dry, but do not let the jib or spinnaker flap wildly, as this will eventually degrade the material.

- Starting at the head, roll the mainsail around the battens (right and below). Roll the jib from the head to the foot. Pack the spinnaker lightly in its storage bag.

- If there are issues with security, remove the rudders, mainsheet assembly, plus principal blocks for the jib and spinnaker.

- If you leave a catamaran with the mast up, you need to tie it down to prevent it being blown over in high winds. Use some form of ground anchor on either side. Spiral stakes or concrete-filled car tyres with attachment points can do the job, as seen in the photo below.

- Trampolines will fade, all materials will eventually degrade in sunlight. Trampoline and hull covers are a very good investment for keeping a catamaran in top condition. Expensive foils are vulnerable to damage on shore. Invest in padded foil bags.

- Use a water-repellent lubricant to ensure free-running blocks and fittings. Replace the shockcord and control lines before they are worn or frayed.

Roll the mainsail round the battens before stowing away

It is a wise precaution to secure your cat to a solid ground anchor

Ready to rock? This could be you in cat action!

10 | Wind and Water

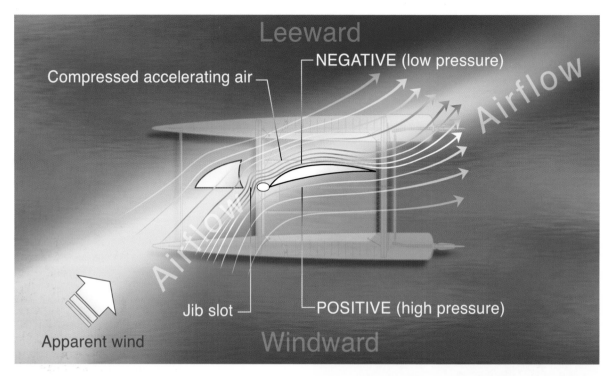

Leeward

Compressed accelerating air

NEGATIVE (low pressure)

Airflow

Airflow

Apparent wind

Jib slot

POSITIVE (high pressure)

Windward

Positive and Negative

Wind flowing over sails is a moving mass of air particles that separate when they hit the leading edge of the sails. The air accelerates faster round the leeward side as it has further to travel. This produces positive high pressure on the windward side (closest to the wind) and negative low pressure on the leeward side (away from the wind), where the air is thinner. The difference between positive and negative sucks the sail and drives the boat as shown in the illustration, with sufficient force to overcome water resistance against hulls plus air resistance against boat and crew.

Optimum angles

The camber (curve) of a sail must be aligned with the apparent wind at the optimum angle of incidence. This is approximately 15 degrees between the chord (straight line between tack and clew) and apparent wind.

If the angle of incidence is greater, airflow will detach from the leeward side, creating turbulence and losing drive. If the angle of incidence is less, the sail will stall as positive airflow ceases on the windward side. Adjusting outhaul and downhaul controls can change the amount of camber and move its position in the sail.

The jib accelerates the air flow over the leward low pressure side of the mainsail. This is a White Formula 20 in action with unusual double daggerboards.

True and Apparent

- True Wind is the real wind experienced by a stationary person or object.

- Apparent Wind is the wind experienced by a moving person or object.

- If a cyclist is cycling at 10 mph into a true wind speed of 10 mph, he experiences apparent wind of 20 mph. If a cyclist is cycling at 10 mph away from a true wind speed of 10 mph, he experiences apparent wind of zero mph.

- True wind and apparent wind speed will never be the same when a catamaran is moving. Apparent wind becomes progressively stronger as a boat changes course towards the wind.

- True wind and apparent wind direction will only be the same if the boat is sailing in exactly the same direction as true wind. On any other course, apparent wind will come from further ahead than true wind. This results from the induced direction of the wind, determined by the boat's forward progress. The faster the boat is moving, the more the apparent wind will move ahead. Therefore craft such as catamarans (and windsurfers) will always have their sails pulled hard in if there is sufficient true wind to sail fast. Whether the course is upwind or downwind, the apparent wind blows from ahead when a catamaran sails at speed.

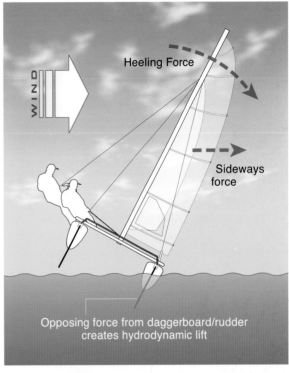

WIND

Heeling Force

Sideways force

Opposing force from daggerboard/rudder creates hydrodynamic lift

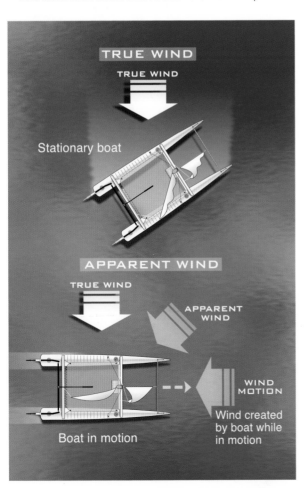

TRUE WIND

TRUE WIND

Stationary boat

APPARENT WIND

TRUE WIND

APPARENT WIND

WIND MOTION

Wind created by boat while in motion

Boat in motion

Sideslip and Lift

A flat-bottomed catamaran would be blown sideways. Centreboards, daggerboards, skegs or a long keel shape (Hobie 16) provide resistance to leeward sideslip combined with hydrodynamic lift towards the wind. The rudder foils also provide some resistance and lift (which creates weather helm), but their main role is to steer the catamaran by deflecting water flowing past when the catamaran is moving. Lifting daggerboards for downwind sailing promotes sideslip. This allows the catamaran to sail a shorter course at a deeper downwind angle, though any advantage tends to be marginal.

Hobie Tiger at full blast on the apparent wind with sails sheeted in on a downwind course.

11 Rights of Way

The basic right-of-way rules are designed to prevent collisions on the water. You should abide by them, but cannot assume everyone else will understand or respect them. Even if you have right of way, it is your responsibility to avoid an impending collision.

Port gives way to starboard

A sailboat on starboard tack has right of way over all sailboats on port tack.

Windward boat keeps clear

If two sailboats meet on the same tack, the boat to leeward (downwind) has right of way. This means a catamaran beating into the wind has right of way over a catamaran sailing downwind on the same tack.

Overtaking boat keeps clear

Overtake without forcing a slower boat to change course.

Power gives way to sail

Be cautious, it is no use being run down while insisting you had right of way.

- There are two important exceptions to these basic rules. Larger craft have right of way if they are 'constrained by draught in a channel'. Commercial craft have right of way over recreational sailors.

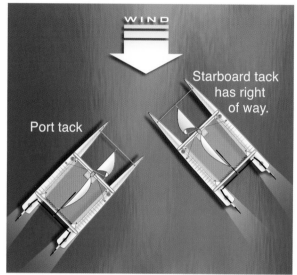

Port tack cat has the option of tacking, stopping or bearing away under the transoms of the starboard tack cat.

Starboard (Guadeloupe second from left) had right of way.

Windward boat (GBR 420) keeps clear.

12 | Points of Sailing

Where can you go?

The three principal points of sailing are beating, reaching and running as shown on the Points of Sailing circle opposite. Catamarans tend to have different characteristics from most monohulls. The big difference is that catamarans like to be sailed fast, all the time. You should always make speed the priority to boost the power of the apparent wind.

The 'No Go' course for any sailboat is directly towards the wind, creating a 'No Go' area of approximately 90 degrees. This is governed by the performance of the boat, how it is sailed and prevailing conditions.

Beating

Beating allows you to sail towards the wind, with a series of zig-zag tacks required to reach a target directly upwind of your position. Most monohulls try to point as high into the wind as possible, reducing the 'No Go' angle to a minimum. Catamarans generally need to be sailed free and fast, pointing at a wider angle to the wind, but more than compensating with their extra speed. Velocity Made Good (VMG) is a compromise between speed and course. Maximum VMG is at about 45 degrees to the true wind.

Reaching

Reaching, with the wind blowing across the boat, is the fastest direction for any sailboat, particularly a catamaran. The rig produces maximum power combined with minimum side pressure. With widely spaced hulls, the crew of a catamaran has the leverage to maximise the power of the rig, which provides forward energy. The relationship between true wind and the speed of the boat means that in any wind speed greater than a very light breeze (around Force 2), the apparent wind will always blow from ahead and increase with the forward speed of the catamaran. Maximum speed is achieved at about 110 degrees to the true wind.

Running

Running in the same direction as the wind is not a good way to sail a catamaran, since it is not possible to build up the power of the apparent wind. Instead, catamaran sailors should sail a zig-zag course to get to a point directly downwind, gybing from reach to reach. The faster the catamaran goes, the tighter the angle of the apparent wind becomes, which enables the catamaran to bear away and sail a lower course. A skilled crew will sail on a reach, build up speed and apparent wind, bear away and be able to sail just as fast on a course that is much nearer to directly downwind. Maximum VMG is at about 135 degrees to the true wind.

Despite appearing to sail into the wind, this cat is sailing downwind at about 135 degrees.

The only direction a cat cannot sail is the no go zone directly into the wind. However sailing directly downwind is highly inefficient in terms of speed, which makes this part of the circle an effective no go zone for cat racers.

Maximising VMG to windward on a Hobie 16 – always go for speed on a cat.

13 All the Fun of the Trapeze

The principal advantage of the trapeze is greater leverage. It also provides the sailor with a better view of what is going on around the boat, in a position that is likely to be more comfortable and less tiring than 'sitting out' on the hull. At speed, being on the trapeze tends to provide a dryer ride, since spray mainly breaks over the boat.

Trapeze facts

- Most catamarans are fitted with at least one trapeze, for the crew. Many catamarans also have a trapeze for the helm, allowing both sailors to 'get out on the wire'.

- Trapezing in bare feet is not a great idea. Best practice is to wear grippy sailing boots that protect the ankles and allow maximum movement.

- The trapeze carries all your weight. Make regular checks that all components are in good condition.

- If the catamaran capsizes while you are on the wire, try to unhook before it goes over. If you are down in the water and still hooked on, don't panic. Knock the ring off the hook, moving your hips forward or up to give a little slack.

- Trapezing on a catamaran is different from on a dinghy. More physical effort is required to get out on the wire from a catamaran's flat platform, but once out you tend to enjoy a more stable ride.

- The harness should be tight but comfortable. Use the multi-adjustment buckles. The harness may loosen up when you are on the wire and require further adjustment.

- 'What is the best way to get in or out on the wire?' The answer is, whatever suits your own style, using the guidelines we have given. As with all techniques, practice makes perfect and speeds up the process.

- Keep your feet close together and also keep helm and crew close together. If helm and crew are too far apart, the boat will tend to 'hobby-horse' across waves, which reduces performance.

- Holding the handle while on the wire is not good practice. The handle takes weight off your feet, increasing the possibility of you being knocked off by a wave.

Spreader bar and adjustable straps are standard on most harnesses. Some top cat racers prefer the traditonal lace-up corset style of harness. This usually has a single hook instead of a spreader which helps save bashed hands when repeatedly sheeting in and out.

Most trapeze systems have a cleat so you can adjust height while sailing on the wire. Some top sailors like Darren Bundock and Glenn Ashby prefer a stainless 'dog bone' which has two fixed rings for high and low trapeze positions. Offwind, the crew moves back and trapezes on the helm's dog bone, while the helm sits on the hull.

Trapezing – Crew

Going out: Sit on the side deck close to the shroud. The jib should be cleated, but hold the sheet loosely in your back hand. Hook onto the ring with your front hand – it should be just low enough to hook in without lifting your body. Slide out over the side of the boat on your backside staying 'low and heavy'. This will pull the trapeze wire taut. Do not ease your weight, or the hook may slip off the ring. Pivot your body toward the front of the boat – this frees up your back leg – and use your back foot and front hand to push your body out in one fluid movement. Supporting and pushing with your front hand makes this easier.

Coming in: Grab the handle, bend your knees, support your body on the wire, and slide back onto the side deck and trampoline in one fluid movement. If you are going into a tack, knock the ring off the hook as you come in. It's wise to say 'Hook off!' so the helm knows exactly when to go into a tack or gybe.

Hook in

Hike over the side

Push out

Straighten legs

Trapeze low

Swing in

Take full weight on the wire

Slide in

Unhook

13 | All the Fun of the Trapeze

Trapezing – Helm

- The helm uses the same trapeze techniques as the crew, but has the added complication of holding both mainsheet and tiller. The most important issue as you go in and out on the wire is to maintain constant mainsheet tension and not change the boat's direction. This requires practice.

- Going out, the natural tendency is to pull both mainsheet and tiller as you go, making the boat bear away. Coming in, the natural tendency is to ease the mainsheet and depower the boat, while pushing the tiller away and making the boat head up.

- Until you feel confident, cleating the mainsheet is one less thing to worry about as you go out on the wire. Put the mainsheet and tiller in your back hand, then hook in and rest the mainsheet and tiller on the hull. Lean on it with your back hand. This will keep the boat sailing straight. Edge your weight over the hull and towards the stern to keep the trapeze wire tight, then get your front foot against the hull and push out, keeping pressure on the back hand to 'lock the rudders'.

- The helm must keep looking forward. Looking down will cause the boat to sail off the wind, causing all sorts of problems.

- When coming back in, hold the tiller and mainsheet in your back hand and then reverse the process, bending your legs to bring you close to the boat to be able to lock down both tiller and mainshee before you come in.

- A quicker technique that requires greater expertise is to let your hand slide loosely along the tiller as you go out and in – if you don't physically move the tiller, the rudders will not change direction in that short space of time.

Grab the hook with sheet in back hand

Hook on and lean back

Hike out

Push out with hand on handle

Make sure tiller is locked

Take sheet in front hand

Coming back in

Weight on the wire and tiller locked

Ready to unhook

Bethwaite system

The advantage of the Bethwaite trapeze system (shown below) is having no hook to damage the boat or catch on something in a capsize. The only real difference it makes when trapezing is to restrict how low you can go. If you attempt to trapeze in a flat position (parallel to the water) the ball may pull out of its socket and dump you in the water, which is not a problem with a trapeze hook-and-ring system. The Bethwaite system is favoured for recreational sailing rather than flat-out racing, where maximum leverage is required.

Moving back

- When the catamaran bears away and sails on a reach, the crew will need to move back along the hull to keep the bows flying, rather than pushing them down. As you move back, the trapeze wire will effectively shorten and lift you into a more upright position. There will also be a much greater forward pull. To combat this, the front leg should be braced and the back leg bent, with the crew's body twisted to face forward.

- The faster and deeper the catamaran is sailing, the further aft you need to go, which may mean standing with feet either side of the helm. The worst thing is to lose your footing and fly forward, possibly all the way round the forestay, which is likely to capsize the catamaran. If you start losing your footing, don't hesitate to grab the helm's shoulder or buoyancy aid until you have recovered your balance. Some catamarans are fitted with foot-straps. Others have a restraining line, which exits from the back beam. Hook this onto your spreader bar to ensure you cannot be thrown forward, but also be aware that you are in a 'locked' position.

Balance, height and position on the wire must be just right – particularly if you are celebrating another win!

13 All the Fun of the Trapeze

On the wire

- Once you are out on the wire, let go of the handle and have complete confidence in the trapeze. It is important to trapeze at a height that feels comfortable – neither too high nor too low. All good trapezes need a system to lift or lower the ring, which can be used when you are out on the wire. This is typically an adjustable-length, two-part purchase led through blocks and locked by a friction cleat. Take the weight on the handle with your front hand and extend or reduce trapezing height with the other hand, ensuring the adjustment line is firmly locked into the cleat before you commit your weight.

- The crew should trapeze flat-out for maximum leverage on a beat. The helm needs to be slightly higher, providing increased vision and better control of the boat.

- The trapeze wire will tend to pull you forward, so you need to pull back. When sailing upwind, the catamaran may pitch (rock longitudinally), which will also upset your balance. Try bracing your front foot against the shroud, with your back leg flexed. The front leg supports most of your weight, while the back leg provides balance. As you get steadier, move your feet closer together, bend your body and lean into the direction where the boat is sailing.

- Get used to moving your weight in and out on the trapeze by bending your legs. If the wind is fluky, you will need to respond to lulls and gusts to keep the windward hull flying at the right height. If both crew are trapezing, it's easier for the crew to keep going in and out on the wire. The helm needs a steady position.

Move back on the wire for strong winds and waves.

Tough toes! Fine if you are experienced.

14 | Launching and Landing

Where to Launch and Land

A gently shelving launch ramp with a hard surface is perfect, but beware of slippery areas. Grass or soft sand is fine with a suitable pair of wheels, and you may need some extra helping hands to pull the catamaran back up. Shingle makes for very hard work and may be impossible without a specially laid track under the wheels. Mud is terrible. Beware of having to pull a catamaran across mud or very soft sand at low tide.

A steep launch ramp can create a lot of problems. For instance, the gradient makes it difficult to control the boat on the way down and a struggle to pull it back up. When launching, the boat may go straight into deep water, which makes it difficult for the crew to hold on and get organised. If there is an onshore wind, a steeply shelving beach will encourage waves to build up and break with a strong undertow.

Wind Direction

Cross-shore wind is perfect for launching and landing. It enables catamaran sailors to reach out and reach back in with minimum difficulty. A wind direction that is marginally cross-onshore or cross-offshore should also work well.

Offshore wind can be surprisingly tricky. The bows are pointing towards the beach and need to be steered offshore. But unless the launch ramp is steeply shelving, there is not enough depth to drop the rudders to make a controlled turn, and not enough space to turn without sailing back onto dry land. The solution is to reverse out, with the two crew sitting on the bows of each hull (as shown below). If the transoms of the catamaran are lifted clear of the water, the crew will be able to control direction by dragging their legs in the water. The rate of progress can be assisted by holding out the jib. When the catamaran is far enough out to turn, get back on the trampoline, drop the rudders and start sailing.

Reverse launch in an offshore wind.

Onshore winds can be very tricky for launching. If the wind is strong, incoming waves make it difficult for the crew to hold the boat. Once sailing, each wave that hits the bows will knock the catamaran sideways, back towards the beach. The technique is to luff up to hit each wave as near to bows-on as possible, then bear away to accelerate and sail fast between the waves, with a diagonal course taking the catamaran progressively away from the shore.

Problems with landing in onshore winds can include surfing in on the waves and hitting the shore too hard. If the waves are big some extra help will be needed to turn the catamaran head to wind, get the wheels underneath and push the catamaran backwards up the slope. Beware of getting side-on to big waves close to the shore. Given a chance, they will roll the catamaran, break the mast and shred the sails!

Getting out through waves needs power, but steering will be impaired if it's too shallow to drop the foils.

Beware of waves breaking on the shore which trashed several cats at Ronde om Texel (the world's biggest cat race) in 2005

Awesome! Sailing Hobie Tigers in and out through breaking waves off the beach at La Torche provided an ultimate test for crews and their cats

Using Wheels

Catamarans use a trolley, which is basically an axle with two wheels and moulded cups that fit the hulls. If the going is soft, you need big wheels! Large-wheeled 'Trax' are the best available and make pushing your catamaran as effortless as possible.

How to put a catamaran on wheels

Crew No.1 lifts one bow while Crew No.2 pushes the wheels underneath. The wheel cups need to be just behind the front beam, in a position where the catamaran is balanced fore and aft. If the going is rough, the wheels can be secured in position by a rope attached to both shrouds.

With wheels under the balance point, it is easy to wheel the catamaran on a flat surface or gentle slope. The best position for the crew is facing forward between the bows, pushing on each bridle.

If you wish to park the catamaran on a hard surface such as concrete or shingle, it will need to be supported or protected at both ends. For the sterns, custom supports that lock onto each transom with shockcord are available for most catamarans, though small tyres or carpet offcuts will do the job just as well. With the stern supports in place, Crew No.1 lifts one bow while Crew No.2 pulls the wheels out until they are in 'park' position beneath the bows but still supporting the front of the catamaran.

When pushing the catamaran around on wheels, pay careful attention to the wind direction. In more than a slight breeze, the bows must always point towards the wind. With no mainsheet attached and no downhaul tension, there will be minimal power in the sail, which makes it possible to have the wind blowing slightly from one side. Beware of the wind blowing side-on to the catamaran, as this may blow it over. If a hull starts to lift off its wheel, you need to change direction and push down on that hull as quickly as possible!

Lift the bow and push under the wheels

Wheel the cat on its balance point

Pull the wheels out when the cat floats

Leave them in a safe place

Launching the Catamaran

When you push the catamaran into the water, go in about knee-deep. Crew No.1 holds one bow while Crew No.2 pulls out the wheels from underneath the hulls and carries them back onto dry land – if the tide is coming in, take care to leave the wheels above the tide line.

While the crew holds the bow, the helm gets onto the catamaran. Be very careful if you have a trapeze hook. Novices tend to heave themselves onto the hull with the hook digging into the side of the boat or deck, where it may do some damage. If you have a problem getting on board, move the catamaran into shallower water. The trapeze handle can provide a useful pull-up. The helm hooks the top mainsheet block onto the tack of the mainsail, ensuring that mainsheet and traveller will run free and tensioning the downhaul as required. If there is sufficient water under the catamaran, the helm will push down the rudder foils. Most have a lift-and-drop system using the tiller bar. It is vital to ensure the foils are fully locked down. If there is insufficient water, it will be possible to sail out to deeper water with the rudders only partly down in a light-to-moderate sideshore wind. But beware that steering will be heavy and unresponsive. The helm indicates which way he or she wishes the boat to go. The crew pushes the bows in that direction, hops smartly onto the windward hull (remember your trapeze hook – use the trapeze handle for a lift), partially lowers the leeward daggerboard or centreboard (if fitted) and immediately unfurls the jib to help the catamaran get away. With the catamaran only moving slowly, the jib may need to be 'backed' on the windward side to make the bows bear away onto the correct course.

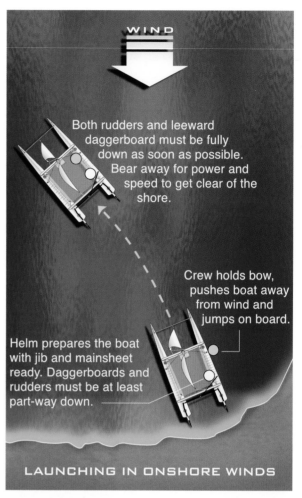

WIND

Both rudders and leeward daggerboard must be fully down as soon as possible. Bear away for power and speed to get clear of the shore.

Crew holds bow, pushes boat away from wind and jumps on board.

Helm prepares the boat with jib and mainsheet ready. Daggerboards and rudders must be at least part-way down.

LAUNCHING IN ONSHORE WINDS

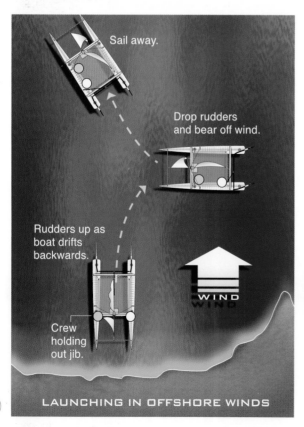

Sail away.

Drop rudders and bear off wind.

Rudders up as boat drifts backwards.

WIND

Crew holding out jib.

LAUNCHING IN OFFSHORE WINDS

Watch out for deep water if launching on a steeply shelving beach

Hold the cat into wind

Crew locks the leeward rudder down

Helm pushes the bows offwind and hops on

Helm and crew ensure both rudders are locked

Crew sheets in and looks ahead

The cat sails off at slow speed

Landing the Catamaran

Coming into shore, the crew furls the jib and gradually lifts the daggerboards or centreboards (if fitted). The helm will lose steerage and control if these foils are fully retracted. Leave some of the leeward foil down until he has steered the catamaran head to wind, bringing it to a halt in water that should be about thigh-level so the rudders can remain down. The crew hops off smartly and grabs a shroud or bow, holding the catamaran into the wind. The helm unhooks the mainsheet and loosens the downhaul to fully depower the mainsail, then lifts both rudders, ensuring they are locked up.

The helm wades ashore to get the wheels, and then pushes them under the catamaran to the 'wheeling' position. At this point, the tyres need to be just touching the ground so that they don't keep moving around in the water – it can be tricky if there are any waves. Start to pull the catamaran back up the slope, paying attention to keeping the wheels in position under the hulls and the bows pointing into the wind. This procedure can be difficult in an onshore wind, when reversing up the beach requires helping hands at the sterns. A useful trick is to lower the mainsail on the water before you come in. Roll it up on the trampoline and sail in under jib alone. You can then furl the jib and pull the catamaran, bows-first, up the slope with no problems due to wind direction.

- Always take a paddle in case the wind drops to a flat calm, plus spare rope in case you need to be towed.
- When launching or landing beware of other beach-users, swimmers and other boats. They probably have no understanding of the difficulties you may have controlling your boat.
- Dropping and rolling the mainsail out on the water requires practice, particularly when unlocking the halyard. Keep trying until you can do the whole procedure with a blindfold.
- A high-quality set of oversized wheels is strongly recommended, unless you usually only launch over perfectly smooth, hard ground, in which case small wheels may suffice.

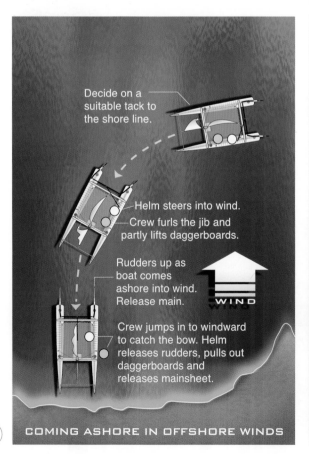

Decide on a suitable tack to the shore line.

Helm steers into wind.
Crew furls the jib and partly lifts daggerboards.

Rudders up as boat comes ashore into wind. Release main.

WIND

Crew jumps in to windward to catch the bow. Helm releases rudders, pulls out daggerboards and releases mainsheet.

COMING ASHORE IN OFFSHORE WINDS

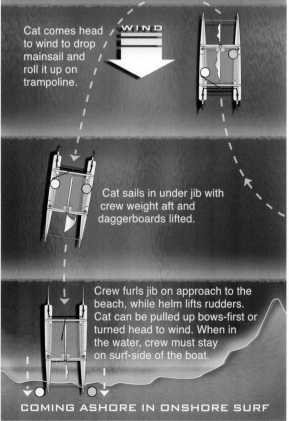

Cat comes head to wind to drop mainsail and roll it up on trampoline.

WIND

Cat sails in under jib with crew weight aft and daggerboards lifted.

Crew furls jib on approach to the beach, while helm lifts rudders. Cat can be pulled up bows-first or turned head to wind. When in the water, crew must stay on surf-side of the boat.

COMING ASHORE IN ONSHORE SURF

Slide the wheels under the cat to recover it from the water, ensuring it is correctly under the balance point just behind the front beam

Always remove the wheels & leave the cat level on shore. A couple of old tyres may be useful to cushion the transoms

15 | Sailing Upwind

Sailing a catamaran to windward requires the best compromise between course and speed. If in doubt, always go for speed, which will also enable you to sail a higher course.

Light winds – up to Force 2

- Light wind is not good for catamarans. The narrow hulls tend to 'stick' on the water with both sterns dragging.

- For maximum performance, the crew must move their weight as far forward as possible, pushing down the bows and lifting the sterns.

- Keep the catamaran sailing free with fairly light mainsheet tension.

Medium winds – Force 2–4

- The catamaran should be sailed with its windward hull just skimming the water. If it lifts higher, the leeward hull will dig into the water and slow the catamaran down.

- Crew weight should be approximately at the mid-point of the windward hull, aligned with the centre of lateral resistance (daggerboard) and centre of effort (fulcrum of the sail). The sterns must not drag and the leeward bow will typically drive through the water at about half-height.

- Crew and helm should trapeze or sit as close together as possible to reduce pitching.

- The mainsheet should be well tensioned, without hooking the leech in a curve to windward.

- The catamaran will naturally tend to luff towards the wind when sailing up a wave. The helm should compensate by bearing away slightly at the top. When trapezing, flex your legs on the way down.

Strong winds – Force 4 and more

- Both crew must move far enough back to prevent the leeward bow from diving too far down.

- The downhaul control is used to progressively depower the mainsail until it is at maximum tension. On a sophisticated rig, this will reduce draught and flatten the top of the mainsail until it has no drive. Derotating the mast can also be used to depower the rig.

- The mainsheet must be eased to prevent the windward hull lifting too high in gusts, then pulled back in to keep the hull flying during lulls.

- In very strong winds, it may help to ease the main traveller a short distance from the centreline, allowing the catamaran to sail free and fast.

Crew control

The crew plays a vital role in high-performance catamaran sailing, handling the mainsheet and downhaul which account for approximately 80 per cent of speed and control.

Sheeting in and out

- Best practice is for the helm to hand-hold the mainsheet on the ratchet block and only use the jammer for short periods – for instance while adjusting the traveller. Pulling the mainsheet through the jammer is a slow method of sheeting in. It is much quicker to pull in a length of mainsheet with your front hand, transfer it to your back hand, which also holds the tiller, bend forward, pull in more mainsheet and repeat.

- A low trapeze position provides maximum pulling power on the mainsheet and makes it easy to drop the sheet in or out of its cleat if required.

- For best upwind performance, the crew should cleat the jib and take the mainsheet with both hands, leaving the helm free to make the best possible job of steering the catamaran through waves. This method is generally recommended as most suitable for high-performance sailing.

Mainsheet tension

Catamarans like a lot of mainsheet tension. If you are not pointing as high as other catamarans, it is most probably due to insufficient mainsheet tension. Check that you can pull the mainsheet in equally hard with both arms – many people find their left arm is weaker. There are two solutions. Either hold the tiller under your back arm or pressed against your neck, so that you have both hands free to quickly haul in the mainsheet. Or pass the mainsheet to the crew, who can use arms and legs to get a lot more pull.

How it feels

- The tiller should feel almost neutral, with just a touch of weather helm (let go and the catamaran will steer towards the wind) to provide precision. If the rudders are not fully down, heavy weather helm will provide an unpleasant sailing experience.

- The degree of weather helm and lee helm (naturally steering away from the wind) can be governed by the length of the tiller bar. Making the bar longer will 'toe in' the rudders so that the leeward rudder always creates weather helm. Making the bar shorter will 'toe out' the rudders and promote lee helm, which is never desirable.

Telltales

Watch the telltales, which should stream back equally to indicate laminar wind flow on both sides of the mainsail. If the inner (windward) telltales start to lift, you must either bear away or sheet in. If the outer (leeward) telltales start to flop, you must head up or sheet out. This holds true when sailing a catamaran upwind or downwind. Due to the twist in the mainsail, telltales at the top will tend to be more 'fluttery' than those lower down.

UNDER-TRIMMING

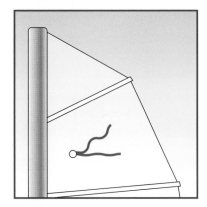

CORRECT TRIM

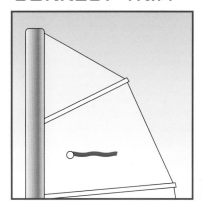

OVER-TRIMMING

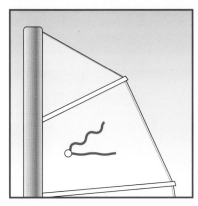

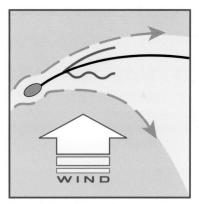

Pull in the sheet

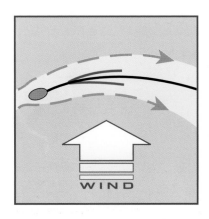

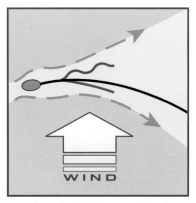

Let out the sheet

Tacking

With two hulls set wide apart, catamarans are slower to tack than similar length dinghies. They tack in a wider circle, since the outer hull has further to turn. All catamarans need to be kept moving through the turn. Some older designs, such as the Hobie 14, are prone to stall halfway through a tack, which requires a 'knack' to overcome. Catamarans with daggerboards or centreboards tend to tack more easily than catamarans with skegs, since they can pivot around the windward foil. If you are sailing in waves, it's always easiest to tack on the top.

1. Check the surrounding water and steer into the tack at speed.

- Be prepared to tack on a windshift. Use visual reference points – such as buildings on the land – to indicate if you have been 'headed' and are sailing a lower course.

- With the rig powered up and the catamaran moving at speed, the helm steers into the tack as the crew comes in off the wire, having sheeted in the mainsail, which is passed to the helm.

- Do not slam the rudders over: they will act like two brakes. Rudders should be pushed progressively as far as possible on a beach cat, however, performance cats with daggerboards only require a 45 degree turn, as they pivot on their daggerboards.

2. Keep weight to windward with the mainsheet pulled hard in.

- Both crew stay on the windward side until the until the jib has 'backed' (filled on the wrong side), keeping the leeward hull light so that the catamaran can spin on the inside. The helm should come in off the wire as late as possible.

- The crew keeps the jib sheeted until the catamaran starts to bear away on the new tack. This is 'automatic' with a self-tacking jib.

- The helm steers the catamaran through the tack, facing aft while moving across the boat and easing the mainsheet by a maximum of about 40 centimetres. This will help the catamaran accelerate and 'pop' the battens on the new tack.

3. On a cat with skegs, push the tiller smoothly as far as it will go.

- The helm bears away as the crew sheets in the jib and goes out on the wire on the new tack. As the catamaran builds up speed, the helm tightens the mainsheet and luffs onto the new course.

4. The crew moves across as the cat turns. The helm pushes the rudders right over.

5. The helm eases the mainsheet when the jib starts to back.

6. The helm pivots across and begins to straighten the rudders.

7. Helm and crew sheet in, with the cat sailing straight on the new course.

Tacking fast is like acrobatics!

Getting out of trouble

• If a catamaran stalls halfway through a tack, it may start sailing backwards. Turn the rudders in the opposite direction and push against the boom. This should reverse the catamaran into the right position to start sailing forwards, with the jib backed to pull the bows round.

• If the wind is light the battens may not pop onto the new tack. Pull down the boom end and push it to windward to force them round.

16 | Sailing Offwind and Downwind

Go for speed

- If you want to sail fast offwind, try to keep the windward hull flying.
- The more it blows and the faster you go, the greater the chance of one or both bows digging a hole. Moving crew weight back is the first line of defence.
- On a twin-wire catamaran, the helm will have better control sitting in, with the crew out on the wire. If it's windy, the crew must have a firm foothold. A rear foot-strap or retaining line can be useful for security.

Traveller control

- The traveller should be eased away from the centreline to remove twist from the leech, as you 'bear away', keeping the mainsail fairly taut to hold the sail's shape. Do not just let the mainsheet out and leave the traveller in the centre of the boat. This leads to bad practice and will damage your mainsail.
- Use your front hand to adjust the traveller position on the track as shown in the photo sequence below, holding the tiller and mainsheet (which may be cleated) together in your back hand. This will power up the top of the mainsail and drive the bows down, as well as possibly damaging the sail.
- It is best to ease mainsheet tension to travel 'up' or 'out'. This takes the pressure off the traveller car and allows easy movement.

When moving the traveller, hold tiller and mainsheet together in your back hand. Let out the mainsheet to allow the traveller car to move easily

Working apparent wind

- The top technique for sailing offwind is to bear away in gusts and to luff in lulls, maximising apparent wind and keeping the catamaran moving at full speed. In big gusts you can bear away until the catamaran is sailing on a true course that is almost dead-downwind, with the apparent wind still blowing from ahead and mainsail and jib sheeted hard in.
- In lighter winds use a wind indicator mounted on the bridle and steer a course at 90 degrees to the apparent wind. If the wind indicator points back, bear away to sail lower. If the wind indicator points forward, head up to build speed.

Reach-to-Reach

If you need to sail a direct downwind course, do not take a straight line. Catamarans get there quickest if they gybe from reach to reach, building apparent wind to maximise speed and the depth of the downwind sailing angle.

If the leeward bow goes down

Sailing on a reach at speed puts enormous pressure on the leeward bow, which relies on buoyancy to oppose the forces pushing it down. The bow is designed to bury under the water and pop out as the buoyancy kicks in. Occasionally this does not work. The bow keeps going down and the catamaran cartwheels into a spectacular capsize as happened to the boys sailing a Hobie Dragoon in the four photos shown below. Tricks to help avoid such an outcome include:

* Sail a catamaran with high buoyancy in the bows, as found on most modern designs.
* Move crew weight back to keep the bows flying. If conditions are challenging, the helm should sit by the rear beam with the crew on the trapeze directly behind.
* Bear away smoothly when changing direction. Do not make a sudden big turn, which will accelerate the boat and drive the leeward bow down.
* Ease the jib sheet to take off power. Ease the mainsheet if necessary. Ease the traveller and do not let the top of the mainsail twist.

Going, going, gone. This cat has clearly passed the point of no return! The result was an inevitable stern over bows capsize

If both bows go down

Sailing at speed deep downwind, both bows can go down and pitch-pole the catamaran end-over-end – but only if you make a bad mistake. This is normally the result of driving the catamaran into the back of a wave, instead of steering carefully over the top. The catamaran suddenly decelerates, with the result that apparent wind suddenly increases and swings behind the mainsail. A combination of momentum and increased force at the top of the sail starts the pitch-pole movement, often throwing the crew forward, which makes the pitch-pole inevitable.

Sailing High and Low

• 'Wild Thing' was developed by Olympic racers to allow the classic two-sail Tornado to sail as deep as possible downwind – with the windward hull flying all the time. It is most effective on catamarans with a daggerboard or centreboard, providing a fulcrum against which the windward hull can push and lift. The trick is to build apparent wind by luffing towards the wind, keeping the hull flying as you bear away. The reduced wetted area of one hull allows the catamaran to sail considerably faster than with both hulls on the water.

• The adoption of the spinnaker means that sailing downwind with the hull flying has become standard practice for high-performance catamaran sailors. Without a spinnaker, standard 'Wild Thing' technique is for the crew to sit on the leeward hull. The helm sets the main traveller close to the leeward foot-strap, sheets in hard, luffs, flies the hull, accelerates and bears away to keep the hull flying on the apparent wind. When the hull begins to drop, the helm luffs to rebuild the apparent wind.

• In some conditions, a few cats may benefit by sailing directly downwind with the mainsheet eased.

Sailing downwind with the windward hull flying has become standard practice for top performance.

1. Gybing from port to starboard, the helm will bear away and push the tiller extension past the clew of the mainsail to the new side.

2. As the helm pivots aft, he will grab the tiller extension with his left hand and falls of the mainsheet with his right hand for a port to starboard gybe.

3. When the mainsheet goes slack, he throws it across the track, pivots round and straightens out the rudders.

4. Power up ready for the next gybe. Always check the whole area to leeward – both in front and behind – before you bear off into a gybe.

Gybing

Don't slow down

Catamarans are easier to gybe than dinghies because the platform is very stable and unlikely to capsize. Problems are most likely to occur if you go into a gybe fast and then slow right down. The result is that the apparent wind will power up the rig at an inopportune moment halfway through the gybe. Maintaining speed throughout the turn is the best way to keep the rig under control.

- The helm must steer carefully through the complete gybe. Do not push the rudders hard over.

- As the catamaran approaches dead-downwind, the helm pivots to the middle of the trampoline on his knees. Keep steering through the gybe. Do not let the rudders 'centre' at the halfway stage.

- The helm flips the tiller extension over and grabs it on the new side, then grabs the falls of the mainsheet with his other hand. When the cat turns through dead downwind, the mainsheet will feel light. At that moment, the helm gybes the mainsail by throwing the mainsheet along the track to the new leeward side, pivoting his body onto the new windward deck.

- The crew crosses the trampoline, avoiding the boom and pulling in the jib (or spinnaker) on the new side, while staying well forward to balance the boat and giving the helm room to move.

- Once the mainsail is safely on the new side, the helm straightens the rudder to correct the course and prevent the catamaran from turning too far into the wind.

- In lighter winds it may be necessary to 'pump' the boom with a quick pull to pop the battens onto the new side.

Going into the gybe, a kneeling position makes it easy for the helm to pivot round to face aft during a tack or gybe.

17 | Spinnaker Sailing

An asymmetric spinnaker or 'gennaker' adds an extra dimension to catamaran sailing and provides a lot of fun for the crew. The extra weight and windage of a spinnaker system will make a catamaran slightly slower upwind, but this is more than compensated for by superior downwind performance, which allows a catamaran to sail at a deeper angle to the true wind. The spinnaker also provides lift, which helps keep the leeward bow flying on a downwind course.

Before you go sailing

It's surprising how many people manage to hoist the spinnaker upside-down or with sheets inside the forestay. To avoid these embarrassments, a dry-land hoist is recommended.

Hoisting the spinnaker

- The crew comes in off the wire for the hoist as the helm bears away onto a broad reaching course. The crew can free the mast rotation limiter, ease the downhaul and lift the windward daggerboard to maximise downwind performance.

- With some spinnaker systems the crew has to pull the spinnaker tack out to the end of the pole before pulling the halyard. With other systems, tack and halyard are pulled together.

- The crew stands on the trampoline to hoist the spinnaker, using the continuous halyard. For maximum efficiency, the halyard is pulled from a shoulder level block on the mast, as used on Tornados and Formula 18 (right).

- While the spinnaker goes up, the helm pulls in slack on the sheet. It is vital that the crew hoists as fast as possible, giving the spinnaker no time to fill before it is fully up.

The helm can 'spot' when the head is pulled as close as possible to the mast. A common mistake is to sheet in and start sailing with the spinnaker when there is half a metre of halyard left to hoist – this will cause bad control problems.

- The crew grabs the sheet, moves back on the catamaran, goes out on the wire and pulls in the spinnaker – all in one fluid movement.

- If the spinnaker is twisted, a few tugs on the sheet will normally untwist the head. If this fails, drop the spinnaker and try another hoist.

Bear away for a controlled hoist which must be as fast as possible to ensure the spinnaker does not get out of control, ensuring it is pulled all the way up.

On the wire or on the boat?

Normal practice when flying the spinnaker on a twin-wire catamaran is for the helm to sit in, with the crew out on the wire. The helm has maximum control while the crew provides maximum leverage on both spinnaker and boat. The crew can spot gusts for the helm, who must know when to ease power in the mainsail and bear away. If you need to sail high with the spinnaker, both crew can go out on the wire. If you need to sail low, both crew can sit in on the boat.

Perfect angles

Sailing with the spinnaker is a compromise between speed to windward and downwind course made good, with apparent wind playing a critical role. You need to experiment to find the perfect downwind sailing angle.

Bearing away

- Bear away progressively using apparent wind to keep the hull flying. Use minimal rudder movement – pulling or pushing hard on the tiller will slow the boat down.
- Mainsheet tension controls twist in a square top mainsail and counteracts the pull of the spinnaker. If you sail downwind with a loose mainsheet, the mast may start to 'pant' with its stop section flexing forward.
- Altering the mainsheet traveller or mainsheet when sailing downwind with the spi is an easy way to break a mast. Safe practice is to set the traveller in the centre and let go the mainsheet so you are not tempted to 'panic ease' the sheet.

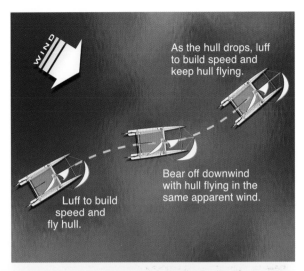

WIND

As the hull drops, luff to build speed and keep hull flying.

Bear off downwind with hull flying in the same apparent wind.

Luff to build speed and fly hull.

Luffing and bearing away is a continuous movement on waves and apparent wind

Wowie! Handling a kite in breaking waves at La Torche is a major test of guts and expertise as these guys are discovering!

Perfect sheeting

For maximum drive, sheet the spinnaker in until the leading edge (luff) is just starting to curl. If the luff starts shaking, the helm must bear away. Do not over-sheet the spinnaker – too much tension will move the draught forward and reduce performance.

Boards up or down?

The spi helps lift the bows, but they still sometimes go down!

- It is theoretically more efficient to retract daggerboards for downwind sailing, but in practice they may stay down. Most Formula 18 crews retract the daggerboards to about half-height when possible. This prevents the sensation of 'tripping' when sailing at top speed with daggerboards fully down, and a full-length daggerboard can snap if it lands on the wrong side of a wave in very rough conditions. It may save time to leave both daggerboards down when hoisting the spinnaker in the heat of a race, and then raise them during a gybe.
- Tornado crews always sail with centreboards down. They are tightly packed to prevent any movement when sailing upwind, which makes them difficult to retract in a hurry. Plus, the Tornado needs to pivot on the leeward centreboard if a quick gybe is required.

Gybing the spinnaker

Gybing the spinnaker is straightforward with the continuous sheet. As the crew comes in off the wire, the helm goes through the same procedure as a conventional gybe: kneel on the trampoline facing aft, steer the catamaran through the turn, grab the falls of the mainsheet and swing the mainsail to the new side. While this is happening, the crew 'pre-sheets' the spinnaker by taking up slack in the new sheet, changes the jib sheet (if not self-tacking) and moves across the trampoline, letting go the old spinnaker sheet and pulling in the new spinnaker sheet in a fluid movement. It requires timing and practice to let the spinnaker blow round the front of the forestay before hauling in on the sheet.

1 Steer into the gybe

2 Pre-sheet the kite

3 Move to the new side

4 Straighten out

5 Sheet in and power up with the apparent wind

17 | Spinnaker Sailing

Dropping the spinnaker

If the catamaran has a chute, you do not have to bear away deep downwind to drop the spinnaker, which was necessary with the old bag-on-the-trampoline system. The crew comes in off the wire, passes the sheet to the helm, uncleats the spinnaker halyard and pulls it down as fast as possible. The spinnaker should slide quickly and easily into the chute with the halyard pulling on three points to ensure it cannot drop into the water.

Pull the kite smoothly and quickly into its chute to ensure it will not drop into the water. If it jams, you may need to re-hoist.

French sailing legend Yves Pajot goes for the drop

18 Capsize

Catamarans do not capsize as easily as dinghies, which is just as well since they are generally more difficult to get back upright after a capsize.

Watch where you fall

If you capsize, the 'top' (windward) hull may feel quite high as the catamaran goes over. Try not to fall into the mainsail, as this may break battens or push the catamaran into complete inversion. It can be dangerous. One catamaran sailor fell head-first onto the mainsail and broke his neck. If you've reached the point where capsize is inevitable, it's best to jump into the water without delay.

Ready to right

- If there is any danger of getting separated from the capsized catamaran, grab a line such as the mainsheet. A catamaran on its side will blow away downwind.

- Do not put any weight on the rig, as this may invert the catamaran.

- Both crew should climb onto the lower hull.

- Make sure mainsheet and jib sheets are uncleated. If you capsize with the spinnaker up, pull it back into the chute before attempting to right the catamaran.

Left: To get a capsized cat into the right position, stand on the bows and wait for it to pivot until the bows are into wind. This ensures that the wind will blow under the rig and onto the trampoline as you pull it upright and that the cat will be pointing into wind as you climb on board. Never right a cat when it is facing downwind, or it may sail away before you can get on board!

Pulling it up

- Most catamarans have a righting line stowed inside a pocket on the trampoline near the foot of the mast. Pull the line out and flip the end over the top hull.

- Both crew lean back on the righting line, until their weight produces sufficient leverage to lift the rig off the water. How easy this is will depend on the size and weight of the catamaran and its rig, the height and weight of the crew and how strongly the wind is blowing onto the trampoline and under the rig. Lightweight sailors can have a problem, particularly when sailing single-handed, and may require outside assistance.

- The rig will start to lift slowly. Once the top hull is past vertical and on the way down, the catamaran will right itself. This can happen quickly. Both crew should drop into the water under the trampoline. Take care not to get hit by the top hull as it comes down! The moment the hull hits the water, the crew should grab the dolphin striker or front beam to hold the catamaran steady. If it is very windy, this may be necessary to stop the catamaran blowing over again in the downwind direction.

- The helm can get back onto the cat by climbing over the rear beam with the tiller bar lifted. However, you may inadvertently bend the tiller some people find this method too difficult. You may inadvertently bend the tiller crossbar, find it too hard to pull yourself through the gap or get a load of bruises. Lack of upper body strength can be a problem. Many people find it easiest to grab both trapeze handles (if you have a twin wire boat), float horizontal alongside the hull, lift one foot onto the deck, pull up on the handles, lift the other foot and roll onto the deck. The helm should ensure the cat is not moving and help the crew on board. Climbing over the front beam is generally not recommended.

Upside-down

In some circumstances a catamaran may totally invert. This makes the righting process slower and may drive the mast into the bottom adding further complications.

- Get on the underside of the trampoline.

- Check all sheets are running free.

- Lead the righting line over the windward hull, then stand at the back of the leeward hull, lean back and pull. This should lift the bow of the windward hull off the water, encouraging the mast to float towards the surface. It will not be possible if the mast has filled with water. Walk your weight forward along the leeward (lower) hull as the windward (upper) hull lifts above you, then continue to right the catamaran as normal.

- Once ashore, check if water has leaked into the mast.

Capsize solutions

- A mast float will stop a cat turning upside down and make it easier to lift the rig off the water. Highly recommended for recreational sailing.

- A 'righting pole' can be fitted to the underside of the trampoline to increase leverage for a single-handed sailor.

- A rescue boat crew can help by lifting the mast tip off the water so wind blows under the rig.

Upside-down in surf is bad

...ially when the mast jams into the bottom and breaks! The solution is to pull the cat up from a capsize fast, before it goes right over.

19 Catamaran Racing

Why Race?

Racing is the best way to improve catamaran sailing ability – sail your catamaran faster, tack and gybe more quickly and keep perfect control. It is the best way to meet catamaran sailing people who can help with practical hints on boat tuning and handling. It also provides the best opportunity to go catamaran sailing as often as possible.

A helicopter signals the start of the famous Rond om Texel race in which up to 700 cats take part.

What is available?

Local clubs with a catamaran fleet organise regular races at weekends and on summer evenings. Catamaran classes stage weekend events for 'travellers' at different venues, plus national championships, which may be held over a full week. Open events are held over weekends for a mixture of different classes. Major catamaran classes run international regattas including European and World championships. The ultimate catamaran racing regatta is the Olympics, staged every four years. In addition, there are various 'long-distance' races. The largest is Round Texel in Holland, which has a maximum entry of 700 catamarans for the annual one-day race. The longest is the Worrell 1000, with an open-ocean course of approximately 1,000 miles on the east coast of Florida.

One-design or open class?

- In a one-design class such as the Dart 18 or Spitfire, all catamarans are exactly the same. Other catamaran classes, such as the Tornado or Formula 18, may have different construction, sails and fittings, but race on equal terms.

- When different catamaran classes race in an open event or long-distance race, a handicap system is required. The ISAF Small Catamaran Handicap Racing System (www.schrs.com) is predominant, although Dutch sailors favour the similar Texel Rating System for the Round Texel Race. Both systems use measurements and specifications to produce rating numbers for each catamaran class.

- Formula 18 was designed specifically for SCHRS. All Formula 18 catamarans must have the same SCHRS number of 1.01, which enables different catamarans such as Hobie Tiger, Capricorn, Cirrus and Nacra Infusion to race on equal terms at all Formula 18 events.

Racing Rules

- Due to the high speed of catamarans it is particularly important to avoid collisions. An impact might not only damage the boat but injure the sailors as well.

- The Racing Rules of Sailing are updated every four years. They are available on the ISAF website (www.isaf.com).

- Fundamental principles are safety, fair sailing and acceptance of the Rules, which are primarily designed to establish rights of way when boats come together.

- The basic Rules Of The Road as summarised on page 56 are paramount when racing:

Rule 10. When boats meet on opposite tacks, port gives way.

Rule 11. When boats meet on the same tack overlapped, windward boat keeps clear.

Rule 12. When boats meet on the same tack not overlapped, boat clear astern keeps clear of boat clear ahead.

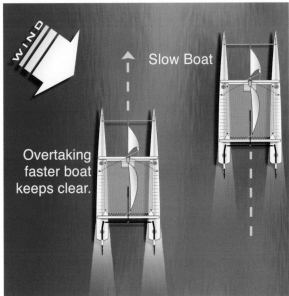

It is vital to know who has right of way in the heat of a race

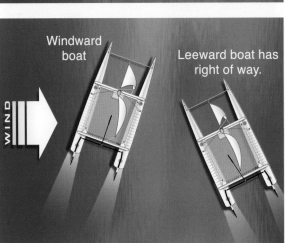

Keep clear when tacking

Rule 13 states 'After a boat passes head to wind, she shall *keep clear* of other boats until she is on a close-hauled course.' Catamarans tack slowly, but you must not tack in another boat's water, which means tacking in front of the other boat and causing an obstruction. The catamaran that is tacking must complete the tack and have its mainsail sheeted in on the new side before the other catamaran has to take avoiding action. Once a cat has completed the tack, Rule12 comes into effect and the other cat has to keep clear.

Mark-rounding rules

Rules become more complex when boats meet at marks of the course, where there is the greatest potential for collision. If in doubt, the best practice is to allow plenty of room and keep clear.

Rule 18.2. 'When boats are *overlapped* the outside boat shall give the inside boat *room* to round or pass the *mark*, and if the inside boat has right of way the outside boat shall also keep clear.'

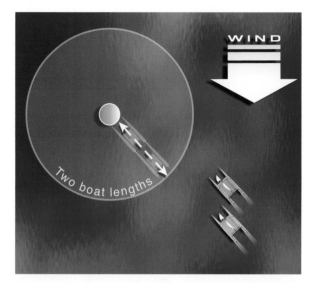

- An overlap is when any part of one boat overlaps the other. If there is no overlap, a boat is clear astern or clear ahead.

- The overlap must be established before the boats enter the 'two-length zone' – an imaginary circle drawn around the mark with a radius of two boat-lengths (approximately 36 feet for Formula 18, 40 feet for Tornado). This ensures that boats cannot barge onto the inside at the last moment while rounding the mark.

- If the inside boat has established an overlap before the two-length zone, it must be given sufficient room to round the mark. This remains true when the inside boat is on port tack and the outside boat is on starboard tack.

Remember the two boat lengths rule. You cannot barge in at the last moment when rounding a mark.

The Race

- Spinnaker catamarans use the modern windward–leeward course, which is mandatory for Formula 18 class racing and Tornado Olympic events. The course is simple, consisting of one leg to windward and one leg to leeward with any number of laps. Catamarans tack upwind to the windward mark and gybe downwind to the leeward mark on a series of reaches which is considerably faster than sailing a direct course downwind.

- The start line is at the bottom of the course – directly upwind. The finish line is at the bottom of the course – directly downwind.

- At the top of the course, a short 'spacer' leg may be used to prevent collisions. This keeps catamarans which have started racing downwind away from catamarans which are still racing upwind in a potentially crowded part of the course. For the same reason, two leeward marks may be used at the bottom of the course. Catamaran crews can choose the port or starboard mark, but must turn from the inside.

Windward–Leeward sequence

The race officer has to balance wind strength and distance to get the right duration, which is approximately 55–60 minutes. If there is good wind the first beat may be well over a mile. Some classes, such as the Olympic Tornado, do this typical sequence twice, but sail round a smaller course.

- Start
- Upwind to Mark 1 (windward buoy).
- Short reach to Mark 2 (spacer buoy) about 50–75 metres distance and slightly upwind of Mark 1. This ensures that catamarans going round Mark 2 and raising their spinnakers do not get in the way of port-tack catamarans that are still beating towards Mark 1.
- Downwind to Gate Marks 3 or 4, which are rounded either as port marks or starboard marks.
- Back upwind to Mark 1.
- Short reach to Mark 2.
- Downwind to cross start/finish line.

Course options

Variations include rectangular, trapezoid, and inverse 'P' courses, which incorporate tight reaching and downwind sailing. Long-distance courses will normally be based on landmarks, such as the Round Texel Race or Fast Cat Race round the Isle of Wight.

The classic course

- The traditional racing course is the 'triangle and sausage', which provides beating, running and reaching. This format is mostly used by traditional two-sail catamaran classes, which do not have an asymmetric spinnaker.

- A typical pattern might be:

Start by 3 at bottom of the course, beat to 1, broad reach to 2, close reach to 3 to complete triangle; beat to 1, run downwind to 3, beat to 1 to complete sausage and cross finish line.

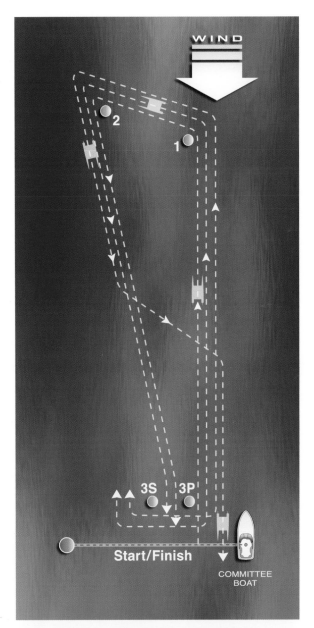

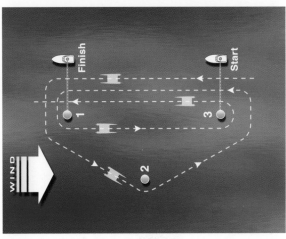

Avoid collisions

- You are duty bound by the Rules of racing to do everything possible to avoid hitting another boat. It is far better to sort out who is in the wrong in the protest room, rather than go through long-winded insurance claims after a crash.

- When sailing to windward on a potential collision course, it is best to push the helm away and crash-tack or stop. If you try and bear away, the catamaran will accelerate, which pushes down the bow. This reduces rudder depth and may lead to loss of steering, with the possibility of cutting the transoms off the other catamaran!

- Sailing downwind, it is vital that the crew scans all round, looking for 'Traffic' as visibility is drastically reduced when the spinnaker is flying. It is always best to bear away early, clearly signalling your intention, to avoid a potential collision.

Sailing at this speed a collision can be dangerous and wreck your boat.

The Start

Laying the start line

- Catamarans normally require a longer start line than monohulls. The general rule is the start line should be equal to the length of all the boats added together + 25–50% to provide a safety margin for different conditions.

- The starter aims for a line that is at 90 degrees to the wind. This angle may be reduced to give port-tack starters a chance when the majority of the fleet will start on starboard tack.

- The reduction for a port-biased line is mostly used to draw the fleet down the full length of the line and avoid committee-boat pile-ups and premature starts. A bias of 5 to 10 degrees works well. Crews who try port 'flyers' need a low heart rate and paid-up insurance policy. The 'door' is often shut firmly on them by starboard-tackers, who get their time and distance right at the gun, while fighting for the pin and pole position.

Start sequences (Racing Rules 26)

Warning 5 minutes:	Class Flag up + 1 sound signal.
Preparatory 4 minutes:	Code Flag P 'preparatory flag' up + 1 sound signal.
1 minute:	Code Flag P down + 1 long sound signal.
0 minutes:	Class Flag down + 1 sound signal.

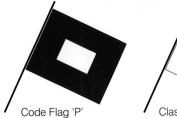 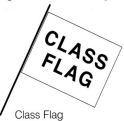

Code Flag 'P'   Class Flag

Leave plenty of time to sail up the first beat and assess conditions on the course in undisturbed wind before the starting sequence gets under way

Organisation

• Starting is often the most demanding part of the race. The aim is for your bows to hit the line as the start gun goes, sailing at full speed with no boats ahead so that you have clean air and can point high upwind. This requires experience, expertise and a very cool head while all around are jostling for position.

• The crew will usually take responsibility for timing the start, checking the committee-boat flags and using a watch that provides reliable count-down information. The crew should also check the tide. Just drop something that floats by a mark and note which way it floats. Beware of a strong current that may sweep you over the start line or against the windward–leeward mark.

• Prior to the first start, check the boat is correctly set up for racing. Cross the line beating to windward at full power and put in a tack. Spot the windward mark if possible. Sail back downwind with a spinnaker-hoist and gybe.

Where to start

• The whole fleet will normally start on starboard tack, with a natural tendency to bunch up by the committee boat. Starting from the committee-boat end has the advantage that you can tack onto port soon after the start, to avoid dirty wind from other boats. This reduces the chance of losing out due to a poor start.

• It is occasionally possible to start from the outer end of the line with a port-tack 'flyer' that crosses in front of the starboard-tack fleet. This high-risk strategy relies on start-line bias that strongly favours the outer end.

• The angle between the start line and wind direction determines if one end is favoured. The start line should be square to the wind, but there will normally be some bias – possibly caused by a late shift in wind direction.

• To assess bias, sail onto the line and turn the boat directly into the wind. If it points towards one end of the line – committee-boat or outer-limit mark – that end is favoured.

• A fleet of boats will often sag in the middle as it crosses the line. Crews at either end have the committee-boat or outer-limit mark to show when they are to the line, which allows them to power off the line the moment the gun is fired. Crews starting from the middle hold back, because they are not sure if they have reached the line. It is possible to use landmarks for reference to confirm the line's position.

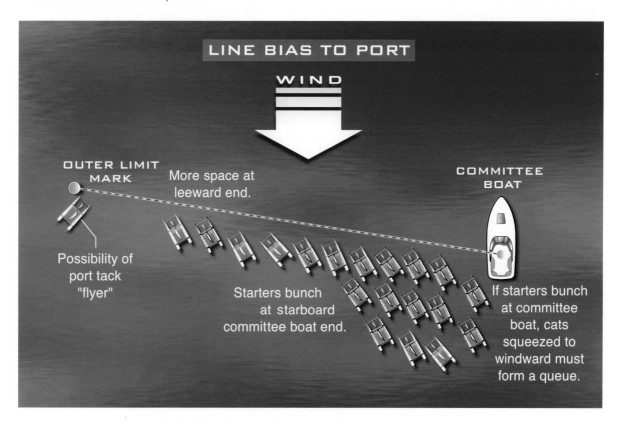

LINE BIAS TO PORT

WIND

OUTER LIMIT MARK

More space at leeward end.

COMMITTEE BOAT

Possibility of port tack "flyer"

Starters bunch at starboard committee boat end.

If starters bunch at committee boat, cats squeezed to windward must form a queue.

The moment of truth as Hobie 16's start a race in the European Championship.

Keeping clear

- A major problem at the start is the turbulence and blanketing effect from other boats. Boats in the 'front' row have clear wind and get away fast. Boats behind cannot point high or sail as fast due to 'dirty wind.' In a crowded fleet this problem may persist for some distance on the first leg of the race. Once clear of the start, boats in 'dirty wind' may have to tack to sail in clean air.

- If possible, keep a space to leeward so you can sail free and accelerate at the start. Boats that are forced to point high will get 'rolled over' by boats sailing across the line at full blast.

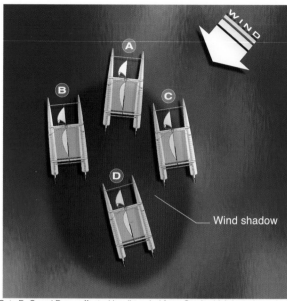

Wind shadow

Cats B, C and D are affected by dirty wind from Cat A which has clear wind

Crossing the line

- In fresh winds it pays to cross the line at full speed. As the final count-down approaches, take up a position around 50 metres behind the committee-boat end of the line. Spot a perfect gap on the line to accelerate through in the last 30 seconds.

- It only pays to sit on the line if the wind is so light that it would not be possible to accelerate through a gap. You must defend your position on the line, holding the boat stationary by pushing out the mainsail and backing the jib. This can also be used to change heading, ready to sheet in and go in the last 10 seconds.

- Do not get pushed over the line just before the start. In the final count-down it's typical for boats to line up in a 'waiting position' ready to accelerate towards the start line during the last seconds. Boats are very close together and may drift very close to the line. If you start drifting over the line, you cannot bear away when a boat to leeward is obstructing your passage – you are the windward boat and you must keep clear. The only solution is to sail over the line, go round the end and rejoin the starters with little chance of a good position.

Starting Recalls (Racing Rules 29)

Rule 29.1 Individual Recall: Used when any part of the boat is over the line on the course side (OCS). The boat may dip back over the line to be on the pre-start side. Code Flag X is flown for individual recalls with one sound signal. The race officer must sound and raise the flag quickly.

Rule 29.2 General Recall: First Substitute Flag is flown with two sound signals to bring all the fleet back. Usually lowered with one sound signal, one minute before the Class Flag to start the sequence again.

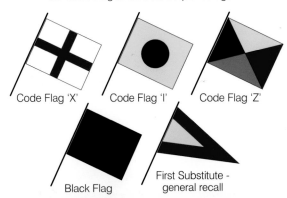

Code Flag 'X'   Code Flag 'I'   Code Flag 'Z'

Black Flag   First Substitute - general recall

Rule 30.1 Round the Ends Rule: Code Flag I is flown instead of Code Flag P with the same time sequence – up at 4 minutes and down at 1 minute before the start. Any boat OCS within 1 minute of start must go around the ends to restart.

Rule 30.2. 20% Rule: If Code Flag Z is flown instead of P, any boat OCS within 1 minute of the start will have its score reduced by a 20 per cent penalty.

Rule 30.3. Black Flag Rule: Black Flag used instead of Code Flag P. Any boat OCS within 1 minute of start is disqualified (DSQ) without hearing.

Windward Leg

Go for speed

- Sail at approximately 45 degrees to the wind for the best compromise between speed and course, known as Velocity Made Good (VMG).

- Catamarans sail very fast to windward but generally tack slowly. (This depends on the design – a Spitfire will tack as quickly as many dinghies.) Tacks should be kept to a minimum, dictated by major wind shifts rather than temporary lulls or tacking to avoid dirty wind from another boat.

Wind shifts and tides

- If the wind is fickle, standard advice is to keep reasonably close to the rhumb line which is a direct route from the start to the windward mark (1). If the wind shifts to the right, the right side of the course is favoured. If the wind shifts to the left, the left side of the course is favoured.

- Tidal currents run slower in shallow water, which is generally inland. If you have to sail into the tide on one tack, be sure to do it where the flow is weakest.

Covering

- 'Covering' is a tactic to ensure a rival boat cannot overtake, usually in the final stages of a race or championship. Boat A positions itself to windward and ahead of boat B, which is stuck in its wind shadow. Boat B tacks to break the cover. Boat A immediately tacks to restore the cover. During this process other boats may get ahead.

The leeward cat is well covered in this Volvo Champions race.

These three cats are overlapped with Seasure in a good position, the leeward cat in clean air and the middle cat held in a sandwich.

Top of the Course

The right approach

- The final approach to the windward mark (1) should be relatively short to allow for wind shifts. Starboard tack ensures right of way; port tack is a high-risk venture.

- Unless you are leading, other boats will be going round the mark at the same time. This will create an area of disturbed air in which you may not be able to sail fast or point high and consequently get pushed down onto the mark. Approach with enough room to leeward to allow for loss of power or dodging other boats, without going so far upwind that you have to reach down to the mark.

- Beware the overlap rule. Do not sail into a space on the inside of another boat within two lengths of a mark.

- The spacer leg may be deep enough to hoist the spinnaker. In Formula 18 the helm usually stays on the wire, while the crew goes in for the hoist. Frequently, it may not be possible to hoist until you have rounded the spacer buoy (2) and turned downwind.

Always go in wide and come out tight at the mark

Leeward Leg

Go for speed

• Sail at approximately 135 degrees to the wind for the best compromise between speed and course, known as Velocity Made Good (VMG).

Shifts and gybes

• If the wind shifts to the right, the left side of the course is favoured. If the wind shifts to the left, the right side of the course is favoured.

• Progress towards the leeward marks is the best indicator of when to gybe. A catamaran will gybe fairly fast, encouraging gybes on wind shifts to sail a shorter course to the leeward marks.

• A fully powered catamaran with a spinnaker can only sail within a limited wind angle. A few degrees too low and it will slow right down; a few degrees too high and it may capsize. This is a particular issue when crossing gybes with other catamarans. Port must give way to starboard – if you have to give way, it may be preferable to gybe out of trouble.

The leeward leg requires maximum VMG with a compromise on speed and course

Do not collide

• When sailing downwind with the spinnaker, beware of boats sailing upwind on the windward leg. You may be sailing very fast with limited ability to manoeuvre; the spray and sails may blanket your view. Sailing downwind, you only have right of way if you are on starboard and the boat sailing upwind is on port.

19 | Catamaran Racing

Bottom of the Course

Mark-rounding

* Beware the overlap rule. Do not sail into a space on the inside of another boat within two lengths of the mark.
* Go in deep and come out tight at the leeward mark. This ensures you can start the upwind leg in the best possible position, with no boat to windward.
* Drop the spinnaker as late as possible. Ensure the daggerboard is fully down on the leeward side before rounding the mark and turning upwind. The helm can go out on the wire while the crew completes pulling down the spinnaker.

Finish

Cross the nearest end of the finish line on starboard tack, unless there are no other boats to contend with.

* Make sure your finish has been logged by the finish boat.
* Post a tally or sign off as required at the end of racing.
* Discuss and analyse the race.
* Fix anything that needs changing.

Race Scoring

The team with the lowest number of points wins a race series overall. Each race counts:

1st place: 1 point.

2nd place: 2 points.

3rd place: 3 points, etc.

DNS/DNC (did not start/did not compete) counts total number of starters plus 1.

PMS (premature start) counts total number of starters plus 2.

DSQ (disqualified) counts total number of starters plus 1.

RET (retired) counts total number of starters plus 1.

Competitors are generally allowed one or two discards in a race series, allowing them not to count their worst results.

Penalties and Protests

* A collision or hitting a mark is a rule infringement. The rule-breaking crew can 'take a penalty by promptly making one complete 360° turn including one tack and one gybe' which should exonerate them.
* If the rule-breaker does not take a penalty, another team may lodge a protest for which they should have strong grounds. Most sailing instructions state that the protestor must notify the Committee at the end of the race. The protestor fills in a protest form and the Protest Committee adjudicates. If found guilty the rule-breaker is DSQ. If found to be a time-waster, the protestor may be DSQ.
* Protests are rare and can lead to bad feeling in a sporting event. Best advice is to avoid them if at all possible!

Keep out of trouble. Do not end up in the protest room by making a silly mistake after all the effort of completing a race.

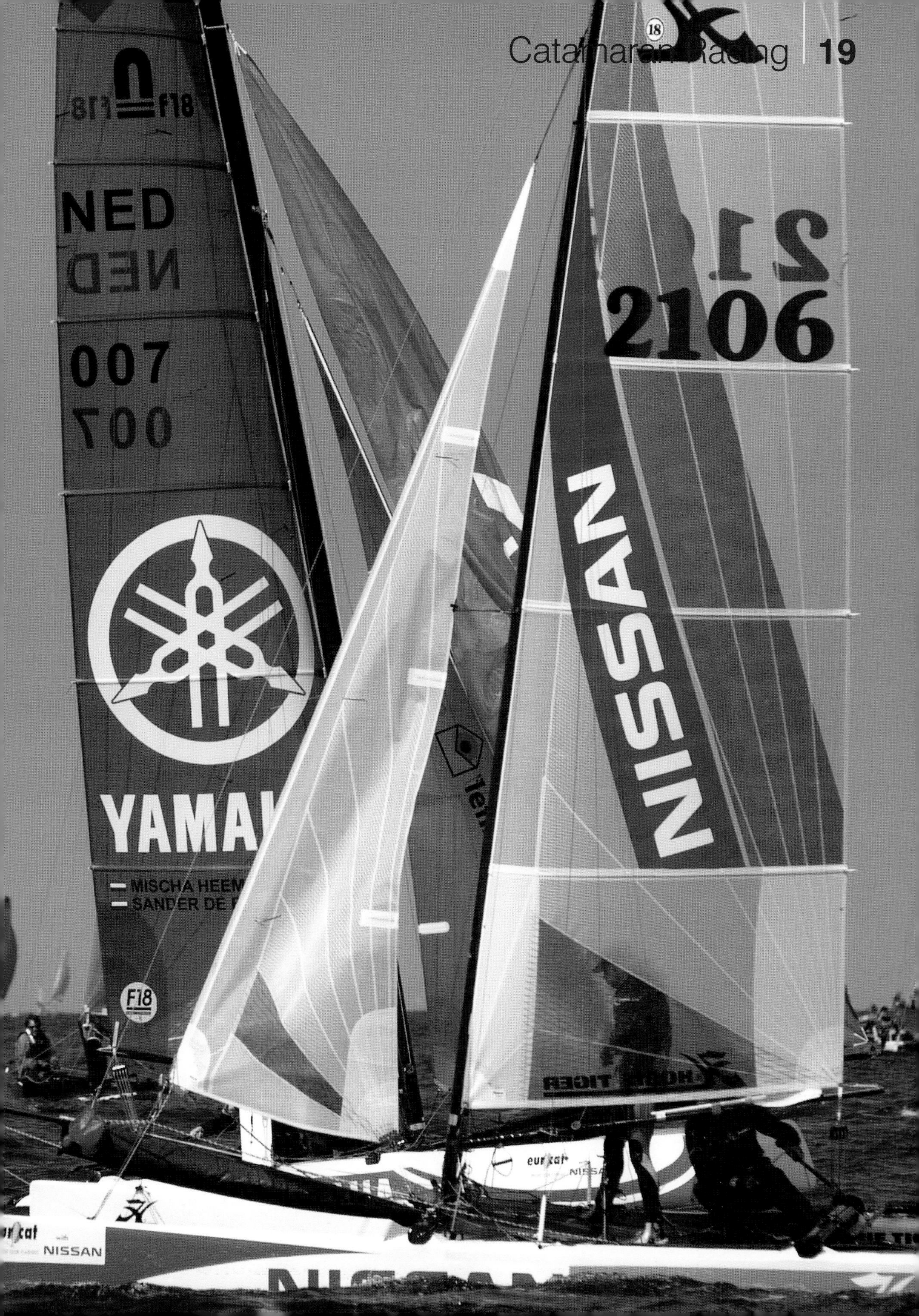
NED
007
YAMA
MISCHA HEEM
SANDER DE
F18
2106
NISSAN
NISSAN

Waiting for the start of the long distance 'Raid' during Eurocat at Carnac, one of the world's major cat regattas.

20 | Round the Course

How do you sail the quickest catamaran round a windward–leeward race course?

Ed Barney (Team Walsh-Barney) and Mark Bulkeley (Team Wilson-Bulkeley) from the Tornado World Class Performance Squad provide the answers.

Setting Up

What are the most important elements of setting up a high-performance catamaran?

"We are sailing against teams that have far more experience and background in the class, such as Mitch Booth and Darren Bundock. To put it into perspective, Bundy won his first World Championship medal the year I was born! So every time we go sailing, we move our understanding of the boat forward. A basic requirement with two hulls is making sure both sets of foils are aligned to limit drag. Understanding how a rotating rig works in line with basic rig settings is crucial. Ultimately it all comes down to time in the boat and becoming more comfortable with which controls do what. For instance, downwind pole height in relation to the kite's luff length is vital – being a few centimetres out will often seriously impinge on our downwind speed."

Ed Barney

"That is a very big subject, which could be broken down into numerous areas, but the basics revolve around getting your mainsail and mast to match and the boat to feel in balance. On a Tornado, we are always trying to set the rig up so we can generate as much power as possible in hull-popping conditions, then look to depower the rig as the breeze increases. As a rough rule you can nearly always depower through use of diamond tension, outhaul and most importantly main Cunningham. It is worth remembering that if you are short of power in the first place, you can't really generate any more. Once you have found this happy medium, it's then a case of fine tuning the rig suit your individual style of sailing, crew weight and the conditions. We normally leave our mast rake alone and use rig tension, diamond tension and battens to accomplish this."

Mark Bulkeley

The Start

How do you win the start?

"Our initial response to this would be 'Good question!' As with any class, there are a few areas that need to be addressed properly and the basics of line bias and space to leeward always apply. Line awareness is crucial on a start line that may be up to 750 metres long for a World or European championship. In relation to this, we always try to have a clear picture of what the boats around us are doing. Knowing when they are sheeting on is vital. Being able to sheet on that fraction of a second early can make or break a race, either providing your first lane upwind or an awful start!"

Ed Barney

"The start in most forms of catamaran racing is a very critical area – the nature of the boats means they are slow to tack, so you want to be minimising tacks on a first beat whilst maintaining clear air. If you get a bad start you will have to tack more and sail in dirty wind, both of which must be minimised if you are looking to round the top mark in the top bunch.

We have developed a pre-start routine that gives plenty of time to gather information such as current, shifts, line bias, transits and which side of the course to choose. Once you have identified all these factors, you need a plan of where you want to start on the line and how you are going to do this. It's then a case of using boat handling skills in the line-up so you've a gap to leeward to accelerate into, plus you need to know where the line actually is. Assuming you have done all this correctly, it's then down to accelerating as quickly as possible to max speed so you can 'roll' the boat to leeward and 'pinch' the boat to windward off.

If you are trying to 'win' an end of the start line – for instance the committee boat end – you need to work out how fast you will drift down the line so you can set up the right distance above the committee boat. You will find it gets pretty busy at the ends. That means you need to be on top of boat control and pretty aggressive with neighbouring boats in order to grab the perfect spot. It is also worth noting that the risks increase as you try to win an end, since you have a higher chance of being OCS or getting shut out. But on the right day the rewards can be substantial!"

Mark Bulkeley

Upwind

What are the most important requirements for making a high-performance catamaran go fast upwind?

"Getting a good balance between the helmsman's steering and the crew's mainsheet trim is important. When we are in sync only tiny tiller and sheet movements are required to keep the hull flying just above the water. Some of this goes back to rig set-up as well."

Ed Barney

"In light winds you need to be very focused on trim of main and jib as it's easy to over-sheet and stall the flow over the sails. It's also important to keep the boat moving, which may require sailing an 'S' course, trying to generate power and then take height when you can. Always think about your weight positioning – too far back can have a big effect, digging the transom in. Once you've got the boat going you need to keep in clear air and look for the wind. The best catamaran sailors always seem to be in more wind than anyone else, which is down to judgement rather than luck!

When you are trapezing and the breeze is up, say 10 knots plus, then it comes down to the relationship between mainsheet, steering and main Cunningham downhaul. The crew will have the mainsheet and should be looking to keep the windward hull just flying, with a healthy level of communication about how the boat feels. Is there too much power? More Cunningham. Is the main strapped and low on power? Ease Cunningham. You also need to decide which mode you want to sail in – height or footing. This can be down to your position on the course, phase of the shift or your particular style of sailing. As in light winds, you need to keep your weight in the right place. As a rule of thumb, move it back as the breeze and waves build."

Mark Bulkeley

How do you divide crew responsibilities? Who does what upwind?

"In a mechanical sense, it's fairly simple and consistent throughout the fleet. The helm has the stick and also plays the Cunningham, whilst the crew takes control of the jib and mainsheet. In terms of tactics, we try to make decisions as a team with the thinking that two brains should be better than one! However, we do break some of the other bits down. Ed will always call the windward mark lay-line and generally the approach to the windward mark, while Andy will do a similar job downwind. We're always clear that one of us will concentrate on making the boat go fast, while the other can take time to look around. The biggest thing is to talk – communication is key! We will always try and discuss scenarios before they happen and be clear about our strategy."

Ed Barney

"In light winds Rob does the mainsheet and steering, while I look after jib trim and compass angles, as well as looking for pressure, shifts and the relative position of other boats. With that knowledge we can talk about what's happening and make decisions accordingly. Rob needs to watch the telltales on the main to trim correctly, so can't afford to look around as much. When it gets windier and we are twin wiring. Rob steers and looks after the main Cunningham, which we lead out to the deck where he stands. I look after mainsheet, jib and compass angles, plus watching for pressure and other boats. We always talk about how things feel with the boat and how we can get it in the fastest groove."

Mark Bulkeley

Do you have special tricks when you tack the boat?

"Going into the turn, it's important to have a low windward hull ride height so it doesn't crash down mid tack. The helm must never let the tiller go as judders in steering will stall the boat. Using a backing line on the self-tacking jib is a good way to swing the bows round, especially in waves."

Ed Barney

"Tacking a performance catamaran is a matter of picking a spot where the bow won't get stopped by a wave and then making a nice smooth turn through the wind. If you hit a wave, the boat stops and you end up doing a three-point tack – not fast! If you don't steer through smoothly the boat can stall, just when you are looking to get the bow down and accelerate out of the tack. We have a backing line that allows the crew to back the jib just as you go through the eye of the wind, which can help swing the bow round.

When the wind gets up and waves build it is important to pick your spot and prepare for the tack well in advance. This requires good helm-crew coordination and then a decisive move to 'Go for it!' As the boat goes into the tack, we try to move our weight back to lift the bow and pivot the boat on the windward transom. It's then time to get across the boat, out on the wire and sheeted in as fast as possible. Ultimately, windy weather tacking requires practice. We often spend a day trying to match race upwind in a tacking dual, which puts pressure on your tacking as well as making practice competitive and fun.

In light winds, the whole process needs slowing down. 'Smooth' is the word that best describes a good tack. Try to keep as much speed on as possible, move across the boat without unnecessary jolts, make sure that the mainsail is eased a little as you come out of the tack so you can squeeze the power back on."

Mark Bulkeley

What issues decide who gets to the windward mark first?

"A good start will get you into the top ten, a good first tack into the correct side of the track will get you into the top five, and boat speed will determine where you are from 1st to 5th!"

Ed Barney

Starting is very important. If you start at the right end, go the right way and sail in clear air, the chances are you will be in good shape. If you get a bad start you can still get to the top mark in good shape, but it requires a good get-out-of-trouble plan and you need to be one of the first to tack out. If you can get out to the right in clear air and hit the starboard lay-line, then you can get back in there. If it is light and/or shifty, you must go the right way upwind and also sail in clear air."

Mark Bulkeley

How do you control a performance catamaran upwind when it's blowing hard with waves?

"Practice! Other than that you can break it down into two parts. Firstly set-up, with the Cunningham being the best control in flattening the mainsail and opening the leech. The jib needs to match this shape, so we will always open the slot by going out on the jib cars and opening its leech by going down on the clew board. On all our jibs, we mark the jib sheeting angle with marker lines from the clew board to different luff heights. This set-up will allow the boat to feel much more controllable and let you concentrate on the second part of sailing in big breeze, which is the in-boat technique. Initially, we will try and slip a lot of mainsail – perhaps as much as 2 metres of mainsheet – to allow the helm to steer around or through the waves. In conjunction it's important to watch the wave sets and know what's coming – for instance if you need to lift the windward hull particularly high for a large wave."

Ed Barney

"Set-up is pretty key here. If you have too powerful a rig you will struggle, no matter how good your technique is. So we set our jib to twist off and flatten, using a combination of clew board and jib car positions, jib battens and jib Cunningham. We then try to flatten the mainsail by outhaul, Cunningham and diamond tension.

Once you are set up right, it's important to keep the boat moving. If you try to take too much height too early, you will stall and slow in the waves. We try to build speed and flow over the foils first, then take height. Depending on the sea state we move our weight back and try to keep the boat in the groove. You need to steer more than usual for gusts and waves and also play a lot of mainsheet. These are the conditions where a fit crew and plenty of practice pay big rewards. Once it gets to 20 knots plus, there are not likely to be many more than half a dozen Tornado teams who are still racing as opposed to surviving! Only practice will allow you to become one of them."

Mark Bulkeley

Downwind

What are the main requirements for making a high-performance catamaran go fast downwind?

"As with all boats, smooth steering matters. This controls the boat's ride height and converts power into downwind speed. In breezy conditions, the crew's ability to trim the kite whilst trapezing hard out of the back strap allows the bow to come up and determines how hard the boat can be pushed. Much of it comes down to practice – having made mistakes, you get to know where the boundaries lie!"

Ed Barney

"Steering downwind must be smooth. It helps if the helm can steer using the tiller bar, which gives a better and more direct feel than the extension. There has to be a balance between steering, spinnaker trim and weight position, both fore and aft and up and down. In light to moderate winds we are always looking to fly the hull and also keep the boat driving forwards. Sometimes you can have the hull flying but the boat doesn't want to go forwards – this is a sign that you need to move the weight up. We always try to keep a good level of chat going about pressure in the sheet, pressure coming down the course and how the boat feels.

When it is windy and the crew is trapezing, it's a case of driving the boat hard, keeping the hull flying and steering through the waves, combined with spinnaker trim to allow the boat to ride the waves. You drive down the wave with sheet on, then ease and steer into the wind to go up the face as fast as possible. If you hit a particularly big wave, you can bring the boat down onto both hulls to give more buoyancy and avoid the bow going down."

Mark Bulkeley

What are special crew responsibilities downwind?

"Tactical calls are a bit more on the spot. General strategy is discussed, but sometimes the helm just reacts to other boats or changing pressure by calling a gybe."

Ed Barney

"Rob steers and does the tactics. Mark looks after spinnaker trim and most of the weight movement, while keeping an eye out for boats and pressure."

Mark Bulkeley

Can you describe your perfect catamaran gybing technique?

"Our in-boat gybing technique varies, depending on wind and wave state, with some ideas that apply throughout. We're always looking for a smooth, consistent curve, aiming to have as much speed as possible going into the gybe. We carry this speed through the gybe so the boat doesn't become loaded in the middle. Having some idea of the amount of pressure to expect when you exit the gybe is important, and will allow the helm to correct his steering so the boat doesn't 'kick' or stall.

In terms of crew work, the most important thing is to always be in control of the kite sheet. As you move onto the trampoline the kite must not flog, which would obviously slow the boat down. So I try to move my hand down the sheet before coming in off the wire, then hold the sheet backwards over my shoulder to keep some tension as I move in. As the boat starts to turn, a quick tug on the current/old spinnaker sheet helps prevent the kite from twisting before pulling in the new sheet and allowing the boat to accelerate."

Ed Barney

"Smooth turns are paramount. You need to experiment in different conditions as to how fast you can steer the boat through, but it must always be a nice smooth arc. The spinnaker should blow through and fill as you pop the battens and accelerate out of the gybe. In light to moderate winds, I stay down out-of-the-tack to promote popping the windward hull, before bringing my weight up to drive the boat forwards. As you go into the gybe you need to ease the kite slowly. Then as you go through the wind, you need a sharp tug on the kite sheet to back the spinnaker onto the jib so it can blow through without 'furling'. Then pull in the new sheet without over-sheeting the kite, which would rob you of power and acceleration.

Things are similar when it's windy and the crew is on the wire, but you need to add the crew coming in off the wire to the mix. It's important to pick your spot and then make a committed turn through the gybe. How fast you do this will depend on your skill, experience and confidence level. We tend to throw the boat through pretty quickly these days. I'm confident enough in Rob's steering that it will be the same each time! Once you have that level of respect you can gybe on demand very quickly. Practice is the key and video can prove a real eye opener with plenty of food for thought."

Mark Bulkeley

What do you recommend as best practice for hoists and drops?

"Hoisting and dropping is somewhat dependent on what system you run. We have a separate tack line to the kite halyard, with a two or three-patch chute being possible options. Having a clear routine for setting the kite is important. With a spreader leg as standard on all championship courses we have time to ease off the downhaul (helm), ease off the jib (crew) and pull the tack line before effectively bearing away. After dumping the mainsheet and bearing away it's just a matter of pulling that kite up ASAP. In any asymmetric class, getting the boat pointing as low as possible makes the crew's job ten times easier. If the helm can manage to get his/her hand on the kite sheet, this helps to make things even quicker."

Ed Barney

"We tend to have a spreader mark, so the reach gives a chance to prepare for the bear-away and hoist. As we go down the reach we will talk about the tactics for the downwind leg. Do we want to straight-set or gybe-set? Have we got other boats around us? Do we want to go high or soak after the gybe? Once we have worked out our plan, we then go for it. Rob will bear away. As he does this, I pull out the tack line so as we round the mark I can jump in and go for the hoist as fast as possible. Once the kite is up, you need to grab the sheet and get the boat moving without delay. If the wind is light, the helm can grab the sheet to help make the kite 'pop'.

Dropping the kite also starts with preparation and chat. We talk about the upwind leg to come, the traffic, our relative position to the downwind marks and which is closer. Once we have decided on the mark we try to leave the drop as late as possible, but we make sure the kite is down as we go round! Sometimes, if we need to leave it very late, Rob will go out on the wire while I finish the drop. The actual mark-rounding needs to be a nice close one that allows you to keep your height on the boats in front. If it is a one-way track, you will need to hold your lane for a long time and a poor rounding will cut down your options considerably."

Mark Bulkeley

What issues decide who gets to the leeward mark first?

"We'd put it down to three things:

1. Good boat speed.

2. A clear lane. It's no use having the best boat speed in the world if you have some numpty sitting right on top of you – vice versa also applies!

3. Your tactical choice means choosing the side with the best pressure or picking the bands of pressure as they fill down. The crew has a very good vantage point when wiring to look around the race track and feed this information back to the helm."

Ed Barney

"Boat speed, pressure and clear air, although a nice healthy lead at the top mark always helps! The first run is a good place to make big gains, especially if you have had a bad top mark position. You need to be pretty punchy with your calls and look to sail the run in good pressure, making use of the clear air you find yourself in, which is the sole advantage of being at the back. The other key area is to plan your approach to the leeward mark – big gains can be made by a smart approach. It helps to have a good grasp of the rules at the leeward mark, talk about your plans and make an aggressive assertion of your rights to other boats. Shout loudly!"

Mark Bulkeley

How do you control a performance catamaran downwind when it's blowing hard with waves?

"It's important to know where the boundaries are. In the Tornado (as opposed to Formula 18) it's easier to lift the windward hull downwind as the breeze increases, but at some point dropping the hull will become the only way to get downwind. Shifting as much weight aft as possible helps to lift the bow. As a crew, it's important to get locked into the back strap so when you hit a bad set of waves you don't find yourself in front of a boat that's pitch-poling on top of you! When sailing in survival conditions downwind, there are two more ways to keep control of the boat. You can either flap the kite sheet, allowing the helm to steer around waves, or over-sheet to slow the boat down."

Ed Barney

"Sailing downwind in big sea and wind, it pays to get weight as far back as possible to keep the bows out. Then try to push it as hard as possible, picking the big waves where you need to back off. It is pretty important to develop an understanding between helm and crew of whether you push or put it down on two hulls. Set-up wise we don't really change anything for downwind in big breeze. The main thing is to keep the boat upright and push as hard as you feel capable. Make your gybes at speed to unload the rig, which will make things easier. Definitely put the kite up, regardless of how windy it is!"

Mark Bulkeley

Stay cool! Trimming to leeward gives the crew a perfect view, but he needs total respect for the abilities of the driver!

21 | Tuning For Top Performance

These tuning tips are based on advice by Mitch Booth (Formula 18 world champion) and Gavin Colby (Hobie 16 world champion) for maximising performance of the Hobie Tiger. They relate directly to Formula 18 with relevance to all high-performance catamaran sailing.

Mast Set-Up

Spreader rake

- Spreader rake corresponds to pre-bend (luff curve) in the mast and can be adjusted to suit crew weight. Straight spreaders provide maximum power. The more spreaders are raked back, the flatter and more depowered the mainsail will be.

- Spreader rake is measured by the direct distance from the trailing edge of the mast to a straight line between the tips of the spreaders.

- The correct amount of spreader rake can only be determined by experience in different conditions. The basic principle is to increase the amount of spreader rake for lighter crews and reduce it for heavier crews, using the following as a guide:

40–54 mm spreader rake for medium–heavy crews in the 155–170 kg range.

55–64 mm spreader rake for moderate crews in the 141–154 kg range.

In excess of 65 mm spreader rake for light crews under 140 kg.

- Spreaders and diamonds support the mast, particularly with the spinnaker. After adjustment, the spreaders must be perpendicular to the mast to ensure the wires stay in place.

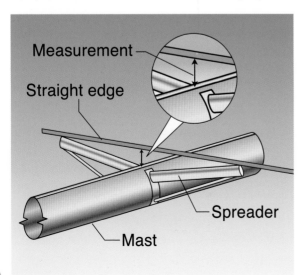

Measurement

Straight edge

Spreader

Mast

Diamond wires

Having decided on suitable spreader rake, it's time to tension the diamond wires. The turnbuckle on the front of the mast can be used to adjust diamond wires for different conditions. The best method is to use a wire tension gauge, obtainable from a chandlery. Wind up the diamond wire tension to depower (increase mast bend). Reduce the diamond wire tension to power up (reduce mast bend). Do not over-tension the diamond wires enough to prevent pre-bend. Preferred tension gauge settings are:

- Under 36 kg for light wind (less than 8 knots).
- 36–40 kg for medium wind (8–18 knots).
- 41–45 kg for strong wind (over 18 knots).

Rig tension

- On a rotating rig, it is important to remember that as the mast rotates the leeward shroud is bearing against the leeward side of the mast. This can create problems when you try to over-rotate the mast for better drive downwind, in particular in light winds when there is no assistance from the sail to push the mast round. Even in moderate winds, the leeward shroud goes slack while sailing upwind.

- Taut shrouds with 30–40 kg tension stabilise the rig. When rigging, each shroud should feel fairly hard if you push with your hand. Loose shrouds will detension the leading edge of the jib, reducing upwind performance. Minimum rig tension is recommended for light winds under 8 knots, steadily increasing rig tension with wind speed.

- If you go too tight, the mast will not rotate freely due to excess pressure on the mast ball and the catamaran just won't feel right.

- Use the mainsheet to pull down sufficient tension when adjusting the shrouds.

Mast rake

- Mast rake can be used to provide the best control, stability and acceleration for different wind strengths or crew weights. Further forward increases power for light winds or heavy crews; further back decreases power for strong winds or light crews. Further back also moves the centre of effort back, which encourages pointing, but may increase weather helm. This can be overcome by raking the rudder blades further forward.

- In a highly powered class such as Formula 18, lighter-weight crews need as much rake as possible. Heavier-weight crews should reduce mast rake in small increments until the boat feels comfortable.

- Trapeze wires can be used to measure mast rake. Take the trapeze forward to the forestay bridle fitting (add line as required) and then swing the trapeze aft until it touches a point on the rear deck. Using this method, maximum rake on a Hobie Tiger is 10 cm from the transom.

Sailing tests

• Test the mast set-up by sailing against other boats. Check for height, speed and power.

• If you are slower through being overpowered – struggling to hold the boat flat and having to point very high – it's probable the mainsail is too full for the crew weight. If you reach the limits of maximum downhaul and reduced rotation (mast rotation lever pointing towards the back of the boat), try increasing diamond tension to bend the mast further. If you are still slow with maximum diamond wire tension, adjust spreader rake towards the maximum.

• This works in reverse. If the boat feels underpowered – not flying a hull and sluggish – with minimal downhaul and maximum rotation (pointing at the leeward shroud), reducing the diamond wire tension will help. But this can only go so far. If the diamond wires become too loose, you risk damaging your mast. Reducing spreader rake is the next stage to straighten the mast, increase sail depth and boost power.

Mainsail

Battens

• Stiff sail fabric such as Mylar or Pentex does not require huge amounts of batten tension. Pull the wrinkles out of the sail and then pull on more tension, starting from the top of the sail.

• The most highly tensioned part of the mainsail is the square top. The top two battens can be changed for different crew weights and conditions. Softer battens produce greater power with more curve in the sail; stiffer battens produce less power.

Downhaul (Cunningham)

• The downhaul or Cunningham is an essential tool since a high-performance catamaran often has more power than is required. Pull it on to flatten the top panels of the sail upwind; let it off to put volume back into the sail downwind.

• As the wind increases, pull on enough downhaul tension to remove horizontal wrinkles from the sail. Then pull more until the luff is flat and firm. In light winds, do not worry about small wrinkles in the luff of the sail – they will not affect performance. In rough sailing conditions, downhaul should be used to limit power for maximum control.

• Downhaul is most effective with stable materials such as Mylar or Pentex. Cross-cut Dacron mainsails on older catamaran classes are more elastic, requiring a longer pull with the downhaul, which provides less precise control.

Outhaul

Outhaul controls foot tension and is a secondary control. Upwind, the foot of the sail should be fairly flat with medium outhaul tension. Offwind, the outhaul can be eased to provide up to 20 cm of camber.

Mast rotation

• Upwind, the mast rotation lever is adjusted to point at the leeward shroud but should be slightly more open than the apparent wind. This will enable perfect airflow over the mast onto the leeward side of the mainsail. In stronger winds, moving the lever aft to point at the traveller will interrupt perfect airflow and reduce power.

• Downwind, the mast rotation lever is let right off so that the mast rotates at 90 degrees to the boat, pushing fullness towards the front of the mainsail.

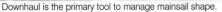
Downhaul is the primary tool to manage mainsail shape.

Mainsheet tension

- Over-sheeting so that the mainsail 'hooks' to windward is a common cause of poor performance. Ensure telltales are flowing, indicating even airflow over both sides of the mainsail. If not, ease mainsheet tension and ensure leeward telltales are flowing smoothly, then increase tension and get the windward telltales to fly evenly.

- The mainsail acts as a backstay when flying the spinnaker. Therefore you must maintain mainsheet tension.

Traveller

- Upwind, the main traveller should be locked in the centre for maximum speed and pointing.

- Offwind, the traveller should be eased a maximum of 30 cm, with full mainsheet tension.

Keep the mainsheet pulled hard in when flying a spinnaker downwind.

Jib

- Use different positions on the clew plate (where jib sheets are attached to the sail) and chain plate (where the tack is attached to the bridle) to achieve a sheeting angle just above 45 degrees.

- Adjust luff tension to suit conditions. More downhaul flattens the jib for strong winds; less creates more volume for light winds. Do not worry about small wrinkles in the luff in light winds. Increase tension to remove wrinkles as the wind builds, then pull on a little more to make the luff flat and firm.

- A self-tacking jib can be locked in different positions on the traveller. Use a tight clew position to close the slot between jib and mainsail for light wind conditions. As the wind increases, use the traveller to open the slot until the boat feels stable, working in conjunction with the mainsail downhaul. The jib should be sheeted on the outer track position for downwind sailing.

Spinnaker

- Make sure the spinnaker will not have a problem when it is hoisted, gybed or dropped. Always do a test hoist before starting a race.

- Ensure all sharp edges, rings and pins are taped over. Turnbuckles and anything that sticks out of the mast must be well covered.

- Spinnaker power can be increased by moving the sheet blocks forward or using deflector blocks to change the sheeting angle. The further forward, the more power is generated. This can be adjusted to suit wind conditions.

Rudder Set-Up

- The pull on the tiller is directly related to rudder rake. If you have too much weather helm (pulling), the rudder blade may need to be kicked under the boat more; if you have neutral helm, it may need to be raked aft.

- The majority of sailors use parallel rudder blades. With the blades vertical, measure the distances between the trailing edges and leading edges at the same height. Adjust the tiller bar until both measurements are equal.

- Parallel rudders may not be fastest. Most catamarans sail with some weather helm so you have to pull slightly on the tiller to keep the boat in a straight line upwind. You could have a few degrees of turn on the leeward rudder, which is fully loaded. The windward rudder has very little load and will only cause drag if it is not aligned with the windward daggerboard. Any amount of toe-in should be kept to the bare minimum. Excess toe-in will harm downwind performance when neither rudder is heavily loaded, and close to parallel is fastest.

Daggerboards

Boards should be fully down upwind and 50–75 per cent up downwind. If the catamaran is overpowered upwind, raising the boards will allow it to 'slip' to leeward and effectively depower the mainsail in gusty conditions.

Hull and Foil Care

Smooth, slippery hulls are fastest! Remove all dings, bumps and imperfections in each hull. Ensure the bottom is sanded to remove any signs of the hull-join and imperfections around the daggerboard case. Polish hulls and foils until you get a reflection, then apply something very slippery with a Teflon base by hand.

Always try the spinnaker before you start a race.

22 Catamaran Care

Hulls & Platform

• General maintenance of hulls is limited to washing off grime. Hulls can be shined up with glass fibre polish. Beware of silicone, which is difficult to remove and may adversely affect future repairs.

• Small chips and scratches to the gelcoat of a glass fibre hull can be made good with a repair kit. It is advisable to get materials from the manufacturer to ensure a correct colour match.

• Check that beams are absolutely rigid – a floppy catamaran is a slow catamaran!

• Trampoline stitching rots in the sun – loose or broken stitching is a telltale sign of imminent failure. Regular checks will pay dividends. Protect the trampoline from UV when not in use. A simple cover will ensure the trampoline stays in good condition for many years. With no cover, the trampoline will fade and deteriorate. Check trampoline tensioning lines for wear and abrasion.

• Check foot-straps and their tensioning lines, every time you sail. Check the fastenings – pop-rivets distort under high loads, the holes elongate with corrosion, the whole fitting pulls out and over the side you go!

• Check tightness of all skin fitting fastenings, such as nuts and bolts for the shroud-plates and gudgeon and pintle fittings on the transom.

Foils

• Most damage to foils is caused by grounding and knocking chunks off the bottom. The trailing edge of a daggerboard may also be damaged by it being pushed back in its case.

• Gelcoat is the correct repair material for a damaged tip or trailing edge on a glass fibre foil. However, it may be too brittle to achieve a strong repair at the thin end of the blade. Marine Filler is similar to Plastic Padding. It is easy to work with, dries in a few minutes and can be quickly sanded or filed close to the original shape, after which the repair can be perfected with fine-grade wet-and-dry sandpaper. It also has the advantage that big repairs can be undertaken with one mixing, while gelcoat requires building up in several thin coats. The principal disadvantage is not getting an exact colour match with the rest of the foil.

• Catamarans with centreboards, such as the Tornado or Hurricane 5.9, have a 'gasket' which seals each case to prevent water pushing up inside. The gasket is a strip of Mylar glued to the bottom of the case with epoxy resin or contact adhesive. A thin line cut down the middle will allow the centreboard to penetrate through, but two individual slot-strips per hull will allow more overlap and greater efficiency. Gaskets should be replaced if they go out of shape with extended use.

• Most rudder systems have a cam mechanism to lock the blade down. This may need adjusting or replacing when:
  1. Blades do not lift on hitting the bottom.
  2. Blades lift when sailing fast.
  3. Tiller has heavy weather helm due to the blade not locking down securely, allowing it to rock fore and aft.

Catamarans get a lot of stress, regular checks and replacement will help ensure you don't end up like the unfortunate guys opposite.

Rigging

- Never go sailing without the shroud adjuster clevis pins and rings properly secured with tape. It's surprising how easily a loose sheet can pull off a ring, after which the pin may fall out. Self-amalgamating tape is recommended for clevis pins. As an alternative, a blob of Araldite will seal them and can be chipped off with a blade if removal is required.

- Check mast attachments for shrouds, forestay, trapeze wires, spreaders and diamond wires.

- All wires should be checked for broken strands. If a strand is broken, the wire is due to fail. Replace it immediately or risk dropping the mast.

- Check for bent or worn pins and fine hairline cracks on shackles used for rigging attachment.

Controls

- Shockcord is used to provide return-tension on many different controls. Replace shockcord as soon as it starts to stretch.

- The traveller should be rinsed with fresh water to remove salt and sand. Do not oil or grease the roller bearings, as they will pick up grit and wear more quickly. The angle of the jammer plate and tightness of the swivel bolt should be checked to facilitate mainsheet jamming.

- Blocks contain ball bearings and should be rinsed with fresh water to remove salt and grit. Do not lubricate the bearings.

Sails

- Wipe sails with a damp cloth to remove marks and dirt. Dacron sails and spinnakers must be dry before being stored for any length of time.

- A Mylar or Pentex mainsail should be rolled around the battens. The best method is to fold down the top three panels, then roll from the head downwards, keeping the battens aligned to prevent warping when stored. Extreme square-top mainsails may need the top battens removed, depending on the angle of the pockets, to allow the sail to roll squarely.

- The mainsail headboard takes a great deal of stress. Check for wear and corrosion, particularly the alloy rivets used to keep the two halves of the headboard fastened.

- Rolling the jib around a suitable length of plastic drainpipe prevents creasing and flattening. The jib luff can deteriorate due to friction with the forestay. Small tears and areas of wear can be repaired with self-adhesive sail repair tape inside the luff tube.

- The jib zip should be checked for missing teeth. Always keep the zipper clear of salt and sand to prevent jamming and corrosion when the sail is left unused for long periods.

- Spinnakers are prone to rips and tears. Always repair a small hole before it becomes a big hole. Self-adhesive spinnaker repair tape is available in a wide choice of colours. It is strong and can be remarkably effective, even when the repair looks messy.

23 | Beaufort Scale

The Beaufort Scale was created by Admiral Sir Francis Beaufort in 1805 to help sailors estimate wind strength. It is still widely used and often exaggerated. The Beaufort Scale is measured in knots (nautical miles per hour – a nautical mile is 2,000 yards.)

Force	Knots	Description	
0	0–1	Calm	Smoke rises vertically. Paddle your catamaran.
1	1–3	Light air	Wind direction shown by smoke drift. Keep paddling.
2	4–6	Light breeze	Wind felt on face. Catamaran will pick up speed but crew must sit by front beam.
3	7–10	Gentle breeze	Wind extends light flags. Leaves and twigs in constant motion. Catamarans can start to fly a hull.
4	11–16	Moderate breeze	Branches are moved. Perfect conditions for catamarans.
5	17–21	Fresh breeze	Crested wavelets form on inland waters. Great conditions for catamarans if you have the skill.
6	22–27	Strong breeze	Umbrellas used with difficulty. The same is true for catamarans. You need to be good to enjoy sailing.
7	28–33	Near-gale	Inconvenience felt when walking against the wind. Don't go sailing – if you're out there, head for shore without delay.

24 Useful Web Addresses

www.a-cat.org	A-Class	www.nacraeurope.com	Nacra
www.catamaran.co.uk	UK Catamaran Racing Association	www.roundtexel.com	Round Texel Race
www.catamaran.ie	Catamaran sailing in Ireland	www.shearwater-asc.org.uk	Shearwater
www.catapultcats.com	Catapult	www.schrs.com	Small Cat Handicap Rating System
www.dart16.com	Dart 16	www.snecca.org	Scotland & North of England Cat Class Association
www.dart18.com	Dart 18		
www.f18-international.com	International Formula 18 Class	www.spitfiresailing.org	Spitfire
www.f18.org.uk	Formula 18 UK	www.sprint15.com	Sprint 15
www.haveahobieday.com	European Hobie Class Association	www.catamaran.de	Topcat
www.hobiecat.org.uk	British Hobie Cat Class	www.tornadouk.com	International Tornado Class
www.hurricane59.com	Hurricane 5.9	www.tornado.org	Tornado UK
www.isaf.org	International Sailing Federation	www.unicorn-cat.co.uk	Unicorn

Glossary

Apparent wind The wind when you are moving.

Asymmetric A spinnaker with longer luff than leech, as opposed to a traditional spinnaker which has equal length sides.

Battens Full length plastic or foam sandwich battens make the mainsail stable under load.

Beach cat General term for a small cat.

Bearing away Turning away from the wind.

Beaufort Scale Traditional wind speed indicator.

Bow Front area of the hull.

Bridle Wire connecting the two bows to the forestay.

Carbon Fibre Very strong laminate material for hull and foil reinforcement. Can be used for spinnaker pole, boom, mast, tiller and similar fittings.

Centreboards Foils which swivel up and down.

Chainplates Adjustable attachment between shrouds and hull.

Chute Tubular chute alongside the spinnaker pole which holds the sail. Can be made in cloth, fibreglass or carbon fibre.

Clew Back corner of a sail.

Code Flag P Preparatory flag for a race.

Course made good Distance to a destination.

Cunningham Alternative name for downhaul.

Dacron Woven material used for sails.

Daggerboards Foils which lift vertically up and down.

Diamonds Wires to control mast bend.

Dolphin striker V shaped reinforcement under the front beam.

Downhaul Control line to tension the luff of the mainsail.

Foam Sandwich Hull construction using lightweight foam core between inner and outer skins which are generally glassfibre, although materials such as carbon fibre may be used.

Foils Rudder blades, centreboards and daggerboards.

Foot Bottom of a sail.

Forestay Front wire which holds up the mast.

Formula 18 International Class of 18 foot cat.

Gybing Changing tacks with the wind behind.

Head Top of a sail.

Headboard Reinforced top of the mainsail.

High Towards the wind.

Jockey wheel Small wheel on the front of a road trailer.

Kite Spinnaker.

Leech Trailing edge of a sail.

Leeward The direction the wind is blowing to.

Leeward mark Bottom of the race course.

Leeway

Line bias When the start line is not perfectly at right angles to the wind.

Low Away from the wind.

Luff Leading edge of the sail.

Luffing Turning towards the wind.

Mylar Laminate material used for sails.

One-Design Cats which are all exactly the same.

Outer limit mark End of the start line.

Outhaul Control for tensioning foot of sail.

Overlap When part of a boat overlaps part of another boat.

Pentex Laminate material used for sails.

Pintles Steel pins for attaching rudder to the transom.

Pitchpole A capsize when the bows dive underwater, usually when sailing fast offwind.

Platform Two hulls, beams and trampoline assembled to form the base of a cat.

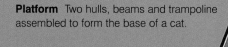

Glossary

Port Left.

Port tack Sailing with the wind on the port side.

Protests Used when there is an infringement of racing rules.

Righting line Thick rope used to pull the cat upright after a capsize.

Rotation Control for changing angle of mast to mainsail.

Rotomoulded Low cost, durable thermoplastic hull construction.

Self-tacking A jib which slides from side to side on a short traveller.

Shrouds Side wires which hold up the mast.

Skegs Shaped fins attached to the hulls to stop the cat going sideways.

Spanner Alternative name for mast rotation control lever.

Spreaders Horizontal struts to control mast bend.

Starboard Right.

Starboard Tack Sailing with the wind on starboard side.

Stern Back area of the hull.

Tack Front corner of a sail.

Tacking Changing tacks with the wind ahead.

Telltales Wool or plastic strips which show how air is flowing across sails.

Tornado Olympic Class cat.

Trampoline Mesh deck between the hulls.

Transom Flat back at the stern.

Trapeze Wire for the crew to hang off, suspended from the mast.

Traveller Slider on rear beam which allows mainsheet to slide to different positions along the full length.

True wind The wind when you are stationary.

Wild Thing Sailing deep downwind flying a hull.

Wind shadow Sails affected by turbulence from neighbouring sails.

Wind shift Wind changes direction which may necessitate a tack or gybe.

Windward The side the wind is blowing from.

Windward mark Top of the race course.

Windward-Leeward course A racing course with just two legs, directly upwind and downwind.

Index

Index

Index

RYA *Membership*

Promoting and Protecting Boating
www.rya.org.uk

RYA *Membership*

Promoting and Protecting Boating

The RYA is the national organisation which represents the interests of everyone who goes boating for pleasure.

The greater the membership, the louder our voice when it comes to protecting members' interests.

Apply for membership today, and support the RYA, to help the RYA support you.

Benefits of Membership

- Special members' discounts on a range of products and services including boat insurance, books, charts, DVD's and class certificates
- Access to expert advice on all aspects of boating from legal wrangles to training matters
- Free issue of Certificates of Competence, increasingly asked for by everyone from overseas governments to holiday companies, insurance underwriters to boat hirers

- Access to the wide range of RYA publications, including the quarterly magazine
- Third Party insurance for windsurfing members
- Free Internet access with RYA-Online
- Special discounts on AA membership
- Regular offers in RYA Magazine
- ...and much more

JOIN NOW

Membership form opposite or join online at *www.rya.org.uk*

Visit our website for information, advice, members' services and web shop.

1 **Important** To help us comply with Data Protection legislation, please tick *either* Box A or Box B (you must tick Box A to ensure you receive the full benefits of RYA membership). The RYA will not pass your data to third parties.

☐ **A.** I wish to join the RYA and receive future information on member services, benefits and offers by post and email.

☐ **B.** I wish to join the RYA but do not wish to receive future information on member services, benefits and offers by post and email .

When completed, please send this form to: RYA, RYA House, Ensign Way, Hamble, Southampton, SO31 4YA

2

	Title	Forename	Surname	Date of Birth			Male	Female
1.				D D / M M / Y Y			☐	☐
2.				D D / M M / Y Y			☐	☐
3.				D D / M M / Y Y			☐	☐
4.				D D / M M / Y Y			☐	☐

Address

Town   County   Post Code

Evening Telephone   Daytime Telephone

email

Signature: _____   Date: _____

3 **Type of membership required:** *(Tick Box)*

☐ ***Personal*** *Annual rate £37 or £34 by Direct Debit*

☐ ***Under 21*** *Annual rate £12 (no reduction for Direct Debit)*

☐ ***Family**** *Annual rate £56 or £52 by Direct Debit*

* Family Membership: 2 adults plus any under 21s all living at the same address

4 Please tick ONE box to show your main boating interest.

☐ Yacht Racing	☐ Yacht Cruising	
☐ Dinghy Racing	☐ Dinghy Cruising	
☐ Personal Watercraft	☐ Inland Waterways	
☐ Powerboat Racing	☐ Windsurfing	
☐ Motor Boating	☐ Sportsboats and RIBs	

Please see Direct Debit form overleaf

Instructions to your Bank or Building Society to pay by Direct Debit

Please complete this form and return it to:
Royal Yachting Association, RYA House, Ensign Way, Hamble, Southampton, Hampshire SO31 4YA

Originators Identification Number

9	5	5	2	1	3

To The Manager: Bank/Building Society

Address:

Post Code:

5. RYA Membership Number (For office use only)

2. Name(s) of account holder(s)

3. Branch Sort Code

	—		—		

4. Bank or Building Society account number

Banks and Building Societies may not accept Direct Debit instructions for some types of account

6. Instruction to pay your Bank or Building Society

Please pay Royal Yachting Association Direct Debits from the account detailed in this instruction subject to the safeguards assured by The Direct Debit Guarantee.
I understand that this instruction may remain with the Royal Yachting Association and, if so, details will be passed electronically to my Bank/Building Society.

Signature(s)

Date

Office use / Centre Stamp

Cash, Cheque, Postal Order enclosed   £

Made payable to the Royal Yachting Association

Office use only: Membership Number Allocated

 077